T0317637

The Ethics of Executive Compensation

The Leeds School Series on Business and Society

General Editor, Robert W. Kolb

The Leeds School Series on Business and Society represents a cooperative venture between Blackwell Publishing and the Leeds School of Business at the University of Colorado. Each monograph volume in this series will address a particular issue or problem area in the broader intellectual arena of the relationship between business and society. As a field of intellectual investigation, we conceive *business* and *society* to embrace the social function of commerce and economic systems, business ethics, and the relationship between business and the natural environment.

The Ethics of Executive Compensation

Edited by

Robert W. Kolb

Blackwell
Publishing

© 2006 by Blackwell Publishing Ltd

BLACKWELL PUBLISHING
350 Main Street, Malden, MA 02148 5020, USA
9600 Garsington Road, Oxford OX4 2DQ, UK
550 Swanston Street, Carlton, Victoria 3053, Australia

All rights reserved. No part of this publication may be reproduced, stored in a retrieval system, or transmitted, in any form or by any means, electronic, mechanical, photocopying, recording or otherwise, except as permitted by the UK Copyright, Designs, and Patents Act 1988, without the prior permission of the publisher.

First published 2006 by Blackwell Publishing Ltd

1   2006

Library of Congress Cataloging-in-Publication Data
The ethics of executive compensation / edited by Robert W. Kolb.
        p. cm.   (Leeds School series on business and society)
    Includes bibliographical references and index.
    ISBN-13: 978-1-4051-3341-8   (hardcover : alk. paper)
    ISBN-10: 1-4051-3341-4   (hardcover : alk. paper)   1.   Executives—Salaries, etc.
    I. Kolb, Robert W.   II. Series.

HD4965.2.E84   2006
658.4'0722—dc22

2005023533
A Catalogue received for this title is available from the British Library.

Set in 10/12.5 pt Dante
by Newgen Imaging Systems (P) Ltd, Chennai, India

The publisher's policy is to use permanent paper from mills that operate a sustainable forestry policy, and which has been manufactured from pulp processed using acid-free and elementary chlorine-free practices. Furthermore, the publisher ensures that the text paper and cover board have met acceptable environmental accreditation standards.

For further information
on Blackwell Publishing, visit our website:
www.blackwellpublishing.com

Preface

On October 29, 2004, a group of scholars gathered in Boulder, CO, for a symposium on "The Ethics of Executive Compensation." Under the aegis of the symposium's title, the approaches and particular areas of concern cover a remarkable range. This could hardly have been a surprise given the diverse backgrounds, educations, and present career missions of the participants. These ranged from business ethicists working in business schools, to philosophers with no special commitment to address issues of commerce, to business scholars who approached the issue of executive compensation from a perspective drawing mainly on the social sciences. Thus the scope of the analyses ranged from studies that analyzed real-world data using canonical statistical techniques to the purely conceptual analysis of values and ethical conduct.

In today's fractured academe in which scholars seldom leave the comfortable confines of their own intellectual silos to explore the surrounding academic land-scape, this symposium created an opportunity for a fertile exchange of ideas across disciplines. Business professors ready to analyze real-world situations and offer guidance to firms met philosophers ready to explore the same issues of concern to conceptual bedrock, and both groups found they could learn quite a bit from each other.

The group was united in agreeing that the present structure of executive compensation is fundamentally problematic from a social and ethical perspective, although their methods, analyses, and prescriptions for remediation stretch the possibilities of the field. The chapters in this volume demonstrate the fruitfulness of broadening the academic perspective to embrace alternative intellectual orientations while bringing them to bear on an issue of genuine social and ethical concern in the conduct of business.

The Japha Symposium is an annual event presented by the Leeds School of Business each fall in Boulder, CO, to address issues of business and professional ethics. CU alumnus and Denver attorney Dan Japha established the ethics symposium in honor of his parents, Lisa and Gerry Japha, through a donation to the Leeds School of Business. In making this gift, the Japha Family's goal was to teach

business students and others in the community the importance of ethical conduct in business and the professions. In addition to the permanent enabling gift of
the Japha Family, we also gratefully acknowledge additional support for the 2004
Japha Symposium from *The Wall Street Journal* and the Boulder law firm of
Caplan and Earnest, LLC.

Robert W. Kolb
Boulder, CO
January, 2005

Contents

Part I: Insights of Empirical Research

Part II: Justice-based Analyses of Executive Compensation

Part III: Broadening the Perspective

Contributors

Carmen M. Alston
PhD Learner, Capella University

Joe DesJardins
College of St. Benedict/St. John's
University, MN

Samuel B. Graves
Carroll School of Management,
Boston College,
Chestnut Hill, MA 02467

Lyla D. Hamilton
Center for Business and Society,
Leeds School of Business,
University of Colorado, Boulder, CO

Jared Harris
Department of Strategic Management
and Organization, Carlson School of
Management, 3-365, University of
Minnesota, 321, 19th Avenue,
Minneapolis, MN 55455

Robert W. Kolb
Leeds School of Business,
University of Colorado, Boulder, CO

Byung-Hee Lee
School of Business,
Hanyang University, Seoul,
Korea 133-791

Jegoo Lee
Carroll School of Management,
Boston College, Chestnut Hill,
MA 02467

Lois S. Mahoney
Eastern Michigan University,
406 Owen,
301 W. Michigan Avenue,
Ypsilanti, MI 48197

Jeffrey Moriarty
Department of Philosophy
Bowling Green State University

Marc Orlitzky
The University of Auckland
   Business School,
Department of Management and
   Employment Relations,
Private Bag 92019,
Auckland, New Zealand

Michael Potts
Associate Professor of Philosophy
Chair, Department of Philosophy
   and Religion, Methodist College,
5400 Ramsey Street,
Fayetteville, NC 28311-1498

William H. Shaw
Professor of Philosophy,
Department of Philosophy,
San Jose State University,
San Jose, CA 95192-0096

Diane L. Swanson
The von Waaden Professor of
  Business Administration,
Founding Chair, *Ethics Education
Initiative*, Department of
Management, College of Business
Administration, Kansas State
University, Manhattan, KS 66506

James Stacey Taylor
Department of Philosophy and
  Religious Studies,
The College of New Jersey,
Ewing, NJ 08628

Linda Thorne
York University, 4700 Keele St.,
North York, Ontario M3J 1P3

Sandra Waddock
Carroll School of Management,
Boston College, Chestnut Hill,
MA 02467

An Introduction

Robert W. Kolb
Leeds School of Business, University of Colorado, Boulder, CO

Executive compensation refers to the total reward provided by the firm to the top level of executives in a corporation, such as the chief executive officer (CEO), the chief operations officer (COO), the chief financial officer (CFO), and a handful of other executives who occupy the very highest level of management. At this level in the firm, total compensation generally consists of many forms that may include any or all of: salaries, bonuses, incentive payments, deferred compensation plans, stock options, and the direct provision of goods and services. In addition to direct cash payments of salaries, bonuses and the like, the other forms of compensation can be relatively large and less visible. For example, stock options granted to executives are not generally visible to the public, yet they may be worth more than the direct cash payments the executive receives. Similarly, many executives receive quite valuable packages of perquisites, "perks," such as apartments, personal staff, personal transportation, and the payment by the firm of many other expenses that most employees would have to bear themselves.

Social and Ethical Issues

Many observers see the size and form of executive compensation as a pressing social and ethical issue. These concerns have become particularly poignant in recent years as the public has become aware of the absolute magnitude and generosity of some pay packages. Further, public attention has focused on numerous instances in which executives have been rewarded very handsomely even as the firms they are supposed to lead have floundered. Public indignation has arisen at the picture of very handsomely rewarded executives coupled with a firm that is experiencing financial losses, facilities closures, and employee dislocations in the form of cuts in pay and benefits and enforced layoffs.

One of the most emotional aspects of this issue is the absolute magnitude of executive compensations. For large firms in the United States, compensation for top executives can run into the many millions of dollars per year. Some celebrated situations have arisen in which compensation for a single year can push toward $100 million, particularly if stock options are granted in that year.

To some observers, the very size of this compensation seems totally inappropriate or even obscene.

Criticism of executive compensation has focused most intensely on practices in the United States, and critics of the present executive compensation practices often point to both domestic and international comparisons to criticize the present level and structure of executive compensation that prevail in US firms. Within the United States, critics of executive compensation point to trends in executive compensation relative to the total pay packages received by rank-and-file employees in the same firm. Most studies suggest that the ratio of executive compensation to that of ordinary workers has increased dramatically in the last few decades. In other words, executive pay seems to be rising much more rapidly than worker pay, and these critics present this data as evidence of a system gone wrong.

Two types of international comparisons play a prominent role in the executive compensation debate. First, executive compensation in US firms appears to be more generous than in comparable non-US firms. Studies have examined the absolute magnitude of compensation internationally, as well as the ratio of executive compensation to ordinary worker compensation across countries. In general, studies find that top executives in US-based companies receive a higher level of absolute compensation (i.e., the actual dollar-worth of the entire pay package) than similarly placed executives in non-US firms. As a second type of international comparison, researchers examine the ratio of executive compensation to the pay of ordinary workers in US firms versus the same ratio in non-US firms. Most studies find a large difference in this ratio, with the executives of US firms receiving a much higher wage relative to that of ordinary workers than would be the case in comparable non-US firms. Again critics take this disparity as evidence of error in the US system.

Defenders of the present arrangement of executive compensation generally acknowledge the overall accuracy of the empirical claims summarized above and grant that executive compensation in US firms is higher than it would be abroad; they also grant that executive pay in the United States has been rising faster than that of workers. These defenders of the present level and system of compensation often argue that trends by themselves constitute no evidence that the present level is wrong or that the trend is moving in the wrong direction. To make such an argument, they assert, merely assumes that previous levels were correct and that recent departures are in error. However, what if previous levels of absolute or relative compensation were too low? Then the movement toward higher executive compensation would be a movement toward a more appropriate level of pay. Similarly, international comparisons might carry little weight by themselves. If US pay levels are high compared to those that prevail in other countries, that might just mean that the other countries have it wrong.

These reflections suggest that the issue must be examined at a deeper level to make real progress in understanding the social and ethical aspects of executive compensation. In particular, a more sophisticated examination of the issue might attempt to answer questions such as the following: Do executives deserve the compensation they receive? Does the present system of executive compensation serve the interest of society as a whole? Does the present level of executive compensation lead to an unjust allocation of a society's resources? Is the present arrangement of executive compensation simply the result of individuals and firms that exercise freedoms and make decisions that rightly lie within their control? Finally, what are the effects on society as a whole of a system in which some receive relatively so much and others so little? The remainder of this introductory essay sketches these issues in turn.

Desert

Could it be that executives deserve the compensation they receive? Top executives of large corporations control the deployment of vast resources in the form of the firm's financial worth, the work of thousands of employees, and even the use of the land and natural resources to which the firm has access. These executives make decisions that have extremely important social consequences. Committing the firm to the wrong investments can waste billions of dollars of wealth, destroy the livelihood of thousands of employees, and even drive the entire firm into bankruptcy. Similarly, the value of correct decisions at this level is gigantic. For example, IBM's decision to create the IBM PC in 1981 spawned an industry that revolutionized work around the world, created any number of related industries and firms, and sowed the seeds of some of the greatest individual fortunes the world has ever seen.

A gifted executive who could make the right decisions at these levels would create value for society that would dwarf even the most lavish executive pay package. Might such an individual deserve very high compensation for exercising his or her talents in a manner that is socially highly beneficial? Many think that the answer to this question is clearly in the affirmative, and they tend to see firms as perpetually engaged in a search for such talent. According to this analysis, it is extremely wise to pay $100 million annually to an executive who can make decisions that would create $100 billion in wealth. Surely, such individuals are rare and difficult to identify, but perhaps the hunt for and competition for those with this kind of potential is justified?

Critics of this desert argument immediately reply by pointing out that actual executives seldom display such genius, and it is in fact easy to identify very highly paid executives who seem much more adept at making wrong choices and destroying value than making brilliant decisions and creating benefits. Beyond pointing out situations in which the actual performance does not seem to deserve high compensation, critics of the desert argument often maintain that no one could merit such compensation no matter how brilliant one's decisions. They argue that it is wrong for any individual to take so much to oneself, no matter how much benefit that individual might create for others.

Freedom

Some view the level of executive compensation as essentially unproblematic no matter what its level, subject to the basic constraints that compensation be determined simply by economic actors exercising their freedom to reach a contract. Here the argument goes as follows: An executive, like any other worker, seeks the best employment contract available. The firm seeks the best managers it can find, subject to its own willingness to pay and the perceived qualities of the potential executive. Both sides of the bargain, firm and executive, merely exercise their basic freedoms as economic actors in a free market and reach an agreement on that basis. As a result, the process is fair and leads to employment compensation that is also fair.

Further, those who emphasize the importance of freedom of contract point out that it benefits society, because the capitalist economic system works by allowing firms to make their own choices and to compete. For the executive, the freedoms being exercised are even more basic than they are for the firm, because the executive chooses to sell his or her own labor.

In rebuttal to this line of argument, critics of the present system of executive compensation assert that the model of two independent agents striking an arm's-length bargain does not describe the situation very well at all, so the emphasis on freedom is misplaced. These critics point out that executive compensation is typically determined by the compensation committee, which comprises members of the firm's board of directors. However, membership in many boards is conferred directly or indirectly by the CEO of the firm. As a result, the very people administering the compensation of a CEO may owe their directors' seats to the very CEO whose compensation they are supposed to judge and control.

Further, top executives and board members are often friends, sometimes old friends of close standing. In addition, many directors serve on the boards of several companies and CEOs of firms often serve on the boards of other firms. This arrangement creates a class of directors and CEOs who flourish in a club-like atmosphere. As a result, the employment contract with the firm's top executive may not be a fair bargain struck by two completely independent parties. Instead, these critics argue, it may well be an arrangement of mutual advantage reached among friends, or at least it may be a situation in which directors are naturally empathetic toward CEOs who are part of the same managerial class. The result of this intimacy, these critics charge, is a set of employment contracts for top executives that is not the result of a pure and free market process, but one of an impure process tainted by ties of friendship or mutual appreciation.

Utility Maximization and Social Goals

Some observers of executive compensation focus on the overall benefits, or overall utility, of the present policy of executive compensation. These thinkers believe that the best approach to such an issue turns on the question of what arrangement will create the highest total societal benefit. As such, they are less concerned with what an executive might receive or deserve, and instead ask what system of executive compensation will create the greatest overall benefit for society. For them, the best system of executive compensation is the one that achieves the goal of maximizing social utility, which we may restrict to the narrower range of social wealth for conceptual convenience.

Even though these thinkers approach the issue from within a framework that emphasizes utility, they can often differ in the solutions they favor because they disagree on the policies that will contribute to utility. One group of thinkers likely to defend the basic structure of executive compensation arrangements approach the issue from the point of view of designing contracts. They analyze the problem in the following terms. The top executives of a firm are agents of the shareholders who are the principals. The executives choose how to deploy the assets of the firm. The perfect agent would allocate those funds just as the principals would desire, were they themselves present and able to make decisions. However, executives are not only agents of the shareholders, but are persons in their own right; thus, their decisions as executives are torn between the pursuit of their own desires and their role as agents of the shareholders.

This conflicted loyalty suggests that shareholders might achieve the best result for the firm by the approach of *incentive compatibility* – making the incentives of the executives compatible with the goals of the firm. The well-designed employment contract allows the executive to prosper when, and only when, the firm prospers. One tool for aligning incentives is the granting of stock options to the firm's executives. The properly structured option in this case is worth very little or nothing when the firm does poorly, but it is worth a great deal when the firm performs well. For example, a stock option given to an executive might payoff handsomely if the stock price of the firm rises by 50 percent over the next 3 years, but may be worth very little otherwise. Under this model, the level of executive compensation is of relatively little importance. Instead, the goal is to structure executive compensation so that the executive acts to create more wealth for the firm even when the executive acts selfishly.

Critics of this line of argument charge that these kinds of arrangements abound in *contracting defects* – the failure of the compensation scheme to align the incentives of the executive and the goals of the firm. These critics point to numerous and well-publicized cases in which executives have been rewarded very handsomely even when the firm suffered horribly. When this happens, these critics protest, the incentives have not been aligned and the result is a failure from the point of view of maximizing utility or the interests of society. As a result, opponents of the present structure of executive compensation still believe that allowing executives to absorb so much wealth diminishes overall utility.

However, merely saying that the present structuring of executive compensation has failed, in fact, to achieve compatible incentives is only a technical argument. It does not yet attack the central intuition of attempting to align incentives, and it is clear that these critics are not merely calling for a technical rearrangement of contract terms. They very much believe that the entire level and structure of compensation is deeply flawed or even evil. While these deeper disagreements over utility and contract design may not have been fully defined, the terms of debate seem to be moving toward clarification.

Distributive Justice

While utilitarian arguments about executive compensation generally concentrate on the total utility effect of compensation arrangements, other critics of executive compensation approach the problem in terms of the distribution of societal resources. For them the issue is not merely the total amount of wealth, but how that wealth is distributed across persons and groups in society. Some critics maintain that the present levels of executive compensation offend against principles of distributive justice. They maintain that a just society is one in which the distribution of wealth, goods, privileges, and positions across society meets certain conditions. These critics maintain that concentrating so much wealth in the hands of these few executives constitutes an unjust distribution of society's wealth and that justice requires new social arrangements aimed at preventing that concentration.

There are many alternative concepts of distributive justice, and different theorists arrive at different principles of a just distribution with radically divergent prescriptions for the allocation of the goods in a society. One sample position on the issue of distributive justice can make the charge against the present mode of executive compensation more concrete by considering *egalitarianism* – the view that the just distribution of goods in a society is one of perfect equality. Egalitarians see the vast gap in wealth between executives and others in society and conclude that such a distribution offends against justice because the distribution is not equal. This egalitarian view resembles that of many distributive justice theorists who believe that a just distribution is one that can be measured only against a particular paradigm. Egalitarians take equality as their paradigm, but other theorists allow for much more inequality and much more flexibility. However, it is fair to say that most of those social observers who focus on issues of distributive justice would be highly critical of the present mode of executive compensation.

In contrast, some reject the very idea that justice might require some particular pattern of distribution. They often argue that any actual distribution that results from processes of exchange that are free from coercion and deception is by its very nature a just distribution. These theorists tend to emphasize freedom of individual action and economic freedom, rather than be concerned about how wealth actually comes to be distributed. As such, they regard the very concept of distributive justice as bogus, at least as it is framed by those who wish to maintain that there is some standard of justice to which the distribution of goods in a just society must conform.

Communitarianism

Communitarian critics of executive compensation argue that the present system harms the community. They tend to see society as a community held together by social bonds in a way that allows citizens to form an organic whole. Extremely high levels of executive compensation place a gulf between a patrician class of executives and the proletariat. As such, this gulf breaks down the bonds of community, weakens society, and works toward a fractured community that is resolved into persons as atoms, unconnected and out of touch with each other.

The remedy for this situation, as far as executive compensation goes, is a system that strengthens the community of executives and workers, a result that can only be achieved by reducing the gap in pay that alienates the two groups from each other. This criticism differs from a focus on utility or distributive justice because it tends to give greater weight to organic wholes – firms, communities, or entire societies – rather than placing so much emphasis on individual persons. By contrast, while those who emphasize utility and distributive justice may agree with the communitarians on policy prescriptions, their concern with utility and distributive justice is still highly compatible with an emphasis on the individual.

Philosophers who take freedom for the individual as a prime value are the natural opponents of communitarians. Against the communitarians, they argue that attempts to build stronger communities by interfering with free contracting of firms with executives tramples on individual rights in a way that is impermissible. Instead, they believe that the right to free action for individuals has a primacy that trumps the pursuit of any social goal, whether it be the maximization of utility, the achievement of some distribution that others might deem to be just, or the building of strong community ties.

Conclusion

Executive compensation continues to attract public attention and generate a lively debate. The lifestyles of executives, made possible by the compensation they receive, cannot fail to generate interest and even envy. The admittedly large gap between executive pay and that of workers is bound to support the continuing view that something is amiss with the system and that some injustice must account for the difference. However, this chapter has attempted to indicate some of the complexity of the issue. Finding the proper solution to the issue of executive compensation will involve the same concepts that arise in the criticism of almost all social arrangements: desert, freedom, utility maximization or wealth creation, the distribution of wealth in a society, and the effects of all social arrangements on the structure and health of communities. The chapters in this volume address all of the issues touched upon here, and they do so from quite different perspectives. I believe that they add considerably to the richness of the debate over executive compensation and help deepen our understanding of this persistent issue.

PART I

Insights of Empirical Research

In "Executive Preference for Compensation Structure and *Normative Myopia*: A Business and Society Research Project," Diane Swanson and Marc Orlitzky explore the relationship between the views of executives on executive compensation and a personality feature that they dub *normative myopia*. A normatively myopic person exhibits "the propensity to ignore, suppress, or deny the role of values in decision-making," a definition that they operationalize and show to be related to a particular preference for structures and levels of compensation. In comparison with traditional philosophical categories, Swanson and Orlitzky locate their analysis firmly within the realm of virtue ethics, as they approach the issue of character in executive compensation. (Michael Potts in his chapter, "CEO Compensation and Virtue Ethics" in Part II of this volume explicitly approaches the issue of executive character in purely philosophical terms.)

For Swanson and Orlitzky, a normatively myopic executive tends to prefer a high level of compensation relative to other employees in the firm. More surprisingly, they show that normatively myopic executives share other personality traits, have similar business educations, and seem to lead firms with chronically poor corporate social performance. Professors Jegoo Lee, Byung-Hee Lee, Sandra Waddock, and Samuel Graves explore the relationship between the financial performance of firms and opportunistic behavior by CEOs in their chapter, "Does Firm Performance Reduce Managerial Opportunism?: The Impact of Performance-based Compensation and Firm Performance on Illegal Accounting Restatements." In general, this chapter finds that performance-based compensation of CEOs tends to increase incentives for the antisocial and unethical conduct of falsifying statements of earnings. While the work of Lee, Lee, Waddock, and Graves is primarily empirical it strikes at the heart of the free-market approach to setting executive compensation.

Even the strongest defenders of a free-market approach to executive compensation recognize the inherent conflict between the interests of the shareholders as principals and the executive the shareholders hire as their agent. In briefest terms, the executive is supposed to operate the firm for the benefit of the shareholders, but the opportunity exists for the executive to use his or her own considerable power and managerial discretion in the deployment of the firm's resources for self-aggrandizement rather than for the benefit of the shareholders. In large part, the executive's employment contract is supposed to resolve this problem by aligning the interests of the executive with those of the shareholders. Thus, "incentive-compatible" contracting schemes aim to resolve the agency conflict and preserve a system in which free contracting leads to wise and ethical firm governance. A key component of such contracts has been employment contracts that compensate the executive based on the performance of the firm, with the idea that the executive will prosper when, and only when, the firm does well.

Lee, Lee, Waddock, and Graves analyze actual firm performance to show that performance-based compensation contracts can actually exacerbate principal–agent conflicts by providing executives with an incentive to submit false earning reports. Thus, far from aligning the principal and agent interests, such compensation agreements may give executives incentives to directly harm the shareholders' interests and to impose huge costs on society generally by lying about firm performance. Even more broadly, this paper raises a greater challenge to the freedom-of-contracting approach to executive compensation: "If employment contract terms cannot be devised to engender ethical and socially desirable executive conduct, how can the freedom-of-contracting approach to executive compensation be defended?"

Lois Mahoney and Linda Thorne also explore the relationship between the executive's employment contract and the conduct of the firms they lead in their chapter, "A Preliminary Investigation into the Association between Canadian Corporate Social Responsibility and Executive Compensation." Mahoney and Thorne explore the relationship between the vehicles by which executives receive their compensation and the conduct of their firms as measured by standard indices of corporate social responsibility. Realizing that even the most well-regarded measure of corporate social responsibility may be subject to question, Mahoney and Thorne find that some of the typical relationships that were thought to exist between firm conduct and CEO compensation may not hold, especially when one considers the size of firms. Thus, firm size, CEO compensation, the salary level of CEOs, the size of bonuses relative to salary, long-term

CEO compensation, and firm performance on standard corporate responsibility measures are all related in quite complicated ways. These results seem to indicate yet more challenges for the freedom-of-contracting approach to executive compensation by showing just how difficult it may be to structure compensation agreements that lead to desired managerial behavior.

1

Executive Preference for Compensation Structure and *Normative Myopia*: A Business and Society Research Project

Diane L. Swanson
The von Waaden Professor of Business Administration, Founding Chair, *Ethics Education Initiative*, Department of Management, College of Business Administration, Kansas State University, Manhattan, KS 66506

Marc Orlitzky
The University of Auckland, Business School, Department of Management and Employment Relations, Private Bag 92019, Auckland 1, New Zealand

Introduction

In our study of 200 executive managers we found evidence of a positive relationship between *normative myopia* and preference for highly unequal compensation structure. In other words, those executives who downplayed the role of values in their decisions generally preferred to be paid extraordinary multiples of the average employee's salary. By comparison, executives who scored low in *normative myopia* preferred more equitable distribution of pay throughout their organizations. Moreover, type of personality and amount of business education helped predict these relationships. We present this evidence in terms of the role of business in society and discuss some implications for research and practice.

In this chapter we summarize our ongoing investigation of executive preference for compensation structure in terms of business and society research (Orlitzky & Swanson, 2002). As background, we began this investigation in 2000 with the support of two university grants. To date, we have surveyed over 200 practicing executives, using an instrument we designed to measure key aspects of decision-making,

This chapter was presented at the *Japha Symposium on The Ethics of Executive Compensation.*

especially *normative myopia* (defined below) and preference for compensation structure (the distribution of organizational salaries). During the course of our investigation, the issue of executive pay has become even more hotly contested, given concerns that excessive compensation at the top of corporate hierarchy cannot be justified in the aftermath of unprecedented business scandals (Thomas, 2004). Some experts worry that extravagantly inflated pay packages ladled with stock options and other rewards have encouraged chief executive officers (CEOs) to be free agents who cash in on short-term gains rather than ensuring their companies long-term prospects (Grossman & Hoskisson, 1998; Altman, 2002).

We are especially interested in how executives view salary stratification in light of the increased disparity that has developed between top managers and the lowest-paid workers during the past four decades (Feenstra & Hanson, 1996; Murphy, 2000). In fact, the ratio of CEO compensation to average workers' compensation is now over 350 to 1 (Rynes & Gerhart, 2000). Obviously, the rising tide in salaries has not "lifted all boats" for employees. Instead, executive managers have benefited disproportionately. This goes to the point of our research project, which is to investigate executive preference for pay in terms of *normative myopia* or the propensity to ignore, suppress, or deny the role of values in decision-making. It is important to know if a positive relationship exists between these two variables. According to the theoretical basis for our study, myopic executives who prefer highly unequal pay distributions can be expected to enact a particularly costly type of poor corporate social performance. That is, they will lead their firms to neglect a host of stakeholder concerns, even while receiving exorbitant salaries. Obviously, this outcome is problematic from a business and society perspective.

To preview the results of our study, we found that executives who scored high in *normative myopia* did indeed espouse a preference for disproportionately large salaries. By comparison, those who scored low favored a more equitable distribution of pay throughout their organizations. Moreover, we found that personality and length of business education highly predicted these relationships. Despite evidence of statistical significance, our findings should be considered preliminary since, to our knowledge, we are the first scholars to explore these relationships in terms of corporate social performance. Hence, the inferences we have drawn need to be validated by future research.

This chapter is organized in three sections. First, we describe the theoretical basis for our study, which is a model of corporate social performance that highlights the role of *normative myopia*. Second, we discuss our survey, which is designed to measure *normative myopia*, preference for compensation, and other factors that influence executive decision-making, including personality and business education. Finally, we highlight some implications of our study for research and practice, including the need to rethink the nature of business education and standards for hiring executives to encourage better corporate social performance or a more constructive role for business in society.

The Theoretical Context of Corporate Social Performance

Normative Myopia *and Corporate Neglect of Social Concerns*

The theoretical context for our study is Swanson's (1999) model of corporate social performance, broadly termed "value neglect." Its overarching proposition is that when executive managers exhibit *normative myopia* by ignoring, suppressing, or denying the role of values in their decisions, then whole organizations eventually lose touch with stakeholder expectations of social responsibility. These expectations, which are value-based, include calls for product safety, respect for human rights, fair employment standards, and sustainable business practices (Swanson, 1999). It can be seen that *normative myopia* and an organizational tendency to neglect social values go hand in hand. Figure 1.1 represents a simplification of Swanson's model.

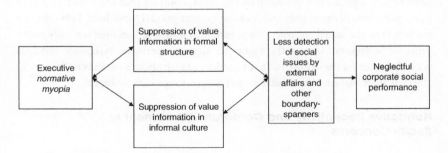

Figure 1.1   Value neglect: executive *normative myopia* and neglectful corporate social performance. Adapted from Swanson (1999).

Its logic is as follows. Executives who exhibit *normative myopia* use formal and informal mechanisms to encourage other employees to follow suit and suppress value awareness and analysis. Formally, executives can do so by using their authority to set a narrow range for employee decision-making along the chain of command structures. Practically speaking, this means that executives can discourage employees from including information about stakeholder expectations in official reports, statements, and other feedback mechanisms. In this way, the range of discretion for subordinate decision-making gets aligned with the narrow value premises set on a higher level of administration (Simon, 1957). Informally, executives can also signal their approval of *myopia* by using certain cultural mechanisms. For instance, they can promote sycophants who convey only desired information to decision-makers and excommunicate or ignore employees who give fuller accountings (Schein, 1992).

The upshot of these formal and informal signals is that myopic decision-making gets replicated among employees, a dynamic that Chikudate (2002) refers to as "collective myopia." When boundary-spanning employees, such as public affairs specialists, align with this shortsightedness, they fail to communicate important information about the social environment to others in the organization (Swanson, 1999). The situation is self-perpetuating in that employees develop a reluctance to convey stakeholder expectations of corporate social responsibility to the executive who signaled disinterest in the first place. Executive and organizational myopia eventually align, as the executive proclivity to ignore or downplay values gets played out as a chronic tendency for the organization to neglect social concerns (see also Scott & Hart, 1979).

As illustrated in Figure 1.1, *normative myopia* and poor social performance are inextricably linked in a theory of *value neglect*. In terms of business and society, *value neglect* represents a violation of the social contract that imputes legitimacy to corporations because they enhance the greater good (Donaldson, 1989). Under the terms of the social contract, corporate responsibilities include not only economizing behaviors but also the ability to forge cooperative, symbiotic linkages with the external environment that function adaptively to sustain life (Frederick, 1995). A firm that manifests *value neglect* fails to forge such linkages.

Normative Receptivity *and Corporate Attunement to Social Concerns*

Essentially, *value neglect* is a benchmark or frame of reference for understanding what can happen to an organization's posture toward society when the chief executive consistently fails to acknowledge and examine the values implicated in his or her decisions (see also Logsdon & Corzine, 1999). In contrast, Swanson modeled *normative receptivity* to represent executive decision-making that consciously strives to include information about values. Accordingly, when executives use formal and informal mechanisms to signal that employees should also attend to values, then the possibility of *value attunement* exists. Put differently, when decision-makers throughout the organization are directed by formal creed and informal examples to recognize and attend to stakeholder concerns, then the organization's posture toward the host environment can undergo a change for the better. In terms of the social contract, cooperation and adaptive, symbiotic linkages become possible.

Although we do not define standards of corporate social responsibility here, *normative receptivity* can be thought of as necessary to a firm's ability to respond constructively to stakeholder expectations. *Receptivity* is the converse of the logic embodied in Figure 1.1 in that it represents an enhanced awareness and appreciation of values in the executive mindset that gets transmitted throughout the informal and formal organization and acted upon by boundary-spanners. In terms of business and society, *value attunement* implies that a corporation has the potential to carry out its part of the social contract described previously.

An Illustrative Example

It is important to note that Swanson modeled *value neglect* and *attunement* as *ideal types*. That is, they represent logical implications drawn from extant research on corporate social performance and organizational theory. In reality, we expect executives to exhibit degrees of *normative myopia* or *receptivity* instead of pure forms of these decision processes. (In fact, our survey, described later, is designed to measure *normative myopia* on a scale from 1 to 5.) Similarly, organizations manifest tendencies toward *neglect* or *attunement* instead of perfect alignments.

To illustrate how *neglect* and *attunement* can be used as points of reference for corporate social performance, consider the long-standing controversy surrounding Nestlé's sales of infant formula. For decades Nestlé Corporation faced social opposition to its marketing of infant formula in developing countries. Critics, including the World Health Organization, claimed that unsanitary water and low rates of literacy rendered the sale of the product unsafe in those countries (Sethi, 1994). Eventually Nestlé was the target of intense pressure from stakeholders aimed at forcing the firm to comply with an international code aimed at restricting such sales. This long-standing controversy can be seen as a clash between narrow profit seeking and broader social values. It appears that Nestlé executives adopted a myopic mindset, referencing narrow company objectives to the detriment of broader community values, particularly a respect for infant life (Swanson, 1999).

In terms of Swanson's models, Nestlé exhibited *neglect*, instead of striving for *attunement* and engaging critics in a timely, constructive dialogue. By adhering rigidly to the original plans, it appears that top executives failed to consider other options. For example, the controversy might have been averted in its early stages if Nestlé had decided to treat the infant formula not as a food product but as a healthcare product, dispensing it by prescription through pharmacies (Husted, 2000). A precedent for this kind of reevaluation already existed in that pharmaceutical companies such as Abbott Labs had successfully responded to stakeholder concerns by making the switch (Austin & Kohn, 1990). That Nestlé was unable to reenvision its identity as a food company can be seen as a failure of executive managers to exhibit *normative receptivity* and factor compelling social values into their decisions.

In this way, *receptivity* and *attunement* can be used as points of reference for underscoring the need for top managers to attend to stakeholder concerns adaptively. Conversely, the logic embodied in *myopia* and *neglect* help explain why social control of business, such as the pressure exerted on Nestlé, becomes necessary in the first place.

Surveying Executives for Clues to Corporate Social Performance

The Main Research Question

Since Swanson's model of *value neglect* highlights decision-making at the apex of organizational structure, it can be extended to include executive traits other than *normative myopia*. Given the trend of exorbitant executive salaries mentioned in the introduction, we are particularly interested to know if there is a positive relationship between *normative myopia* and executive preference for highly stratified pay. Again, such a relationship would connote a particularly costly type of poor corporate social performance in that executives would be paid extravagantly to neglect stakeholder concerns. In this sense, it is worth knowing if executives who favor the highest salaries (relative to other employees) are more insensitive to stakeholder concerns than executives who prefer more equitable pay distributions.

Project Parameters

Given our research question, we designed a survey to measure *normative myopia* and preference for compensation structure. In it, we included several control variables, such as educational background, personality traits, gender, and demographic information. We administered this survey to over 200 practicing managers enrolled in an executive MBA program in Australia from 2001 to 2003.

Although our sample population was confined to Australia, it can be argued that our findings are highly relevant to executives in the United States. According to Hofstede's (2001) well-known cultural comparisons, Australia is the country most similar to the United States in individualism and power distance. In fact, no other countries score as closely on these dimensions. The shared emphasis on individualism equates to a preference for personal initiative rather than an emotional dependence on a community of others that marks collectivism. The similar scores on power distance mean that both cultures tend to justify power distance or inequities in prestige, wealth, and status by expertise legitimized through reward systems. The two countries are also very close in masculinity and uncertainty avoidance, the former denoting a predominant socialization pattern for men to appear autonomous, aggressive, and dominant and for females to appear nurturing, helpful, humble, and affiliating. That both cultures score similarly in uncertainty avoidance translates into a relatively high tolerance for ambiguity and informal work arrangements (Hofstede, 1980).

In the final analysis, a preference for individualism (versus collectivism) is believed to have the greatest impact on management practice (Hoppe, 2004; Triandis, 2004). Given the cultural affinity between Australia and the United States in this area, as well as the other similarities, we can generalize our findings to a US population of executives with a high degree of confidence, keeping in mind that we are in the preliminary stages of research.

Core Variables: Normative Myopia *and* Preference for Compensation Structure

Statistically, the responses to our survey revealed a positive relationship between *normative myopia* and preference for highly unequal compensation structure. This means that the majority of executives who scored high on *myopia* also expressed a preference for highly stratified pay in their organizations.[1] In fact, among the quarter of respondents receiving the highest scores for *normative myopia*, 67 percent also preferred highly differentiated compensation structures. Conversely, the majority of executives who scored high on *normative receptivity* (measured as the reverse score of *myopia*) espoused a preference for more egalitarian compensation. More specifically, receptive executives were shown to reject high pay differentiation in their organizations ($r = -0.23$) and, instead, endorse more egalitarian compensation structures ($r = -0.22$).

To glean more clues about these scores, we asked our respondents to supplement their choices on a Likert scale with narrative justifications. The most common one for pay inequalities was an appeal to self-interest, especially the expectation of a commensurate payoff for an investment in higher education. This response was not surprising, given that our respondents were enrolled in a fairly expensive Executive MBA Program. Yet it was interesting to discover that those executives who preferred greater pay inequalities expressed little concern that income gaps between the highest and lowest employees would become unfair over time. Instead, many referred to the market as the appropriate mechanism for arbitrating increased inequities in pay. By comparison, those executives who espoused more egalitarian pay frequently justified this inclination by pointing to exaggerated differences in salaries as unjust. Moreover, this group expressed skepticism that market forces legitimated large income disparities. One even went as far as to cite Sting, writing, "I want everyone to live in a mansion" and including the word "socialist" in parenthesis. Others invoked norms of community and social justice.

---

[1] The discussant of this paper, Professor Robert Phillips, has observed that "economic values are still values" (Phillips, 2004). Professor Phillips' concern is that our method implies that managers who focus on economic objectives are ignoring or suppressing values. Actually, we draw no such conclusion. While we strongly agree with the assertion that economic goals represent values, we deliberately omitted such definitions and distinctions from our survey. Instead, our aim was to tap executives' attitudes toward values however they might define them. From this perspective, executives who prize economizing do not necessarily recognize it as a value, especially since business education relies on a variant of economic theory that purports to be value free. Similarly, executives might not recognize greed and opportunism as self-aggrandizing values. In essence, we have documented executive self-reported attitudes toward values. As such, we did not investigate any value relationships in the mind of our executive respondents. Indeed, those who reported that values and ethics have no place in their decision-making signaled that they saw no reason to identify and understand such relationships.

Antecedent Variables: Personality and Business Education

Although the executives who exhibited *myopia* tended to invoke self-interest, we did not treat these concepts as equivalent. More precisely, Swanson did not equate *normative myopia* with self-interest *per se*. Similarly, she did not conflate *normative receptivity* with a concern for community and social justice. Although we suspected that there were affinities between *myopia* and self-interest on the one hand and *receptivity* and concern for community on the other, we did not collapse them into single constructs. We did, however, examine the influence of personality and business education on *normative myopia*. In doing so, we found evidence that concern for community (caring for others) and narrow self-interest influenced our measurements through these two predictors of *normative myopia*. We examine the role of personality first.

The Role of Personality

In the widely accepted "Five Factor" model of personality, the following traits are delineated: sociability, conscientiousness, agreeableness, emotional stability, and intellectual openness to experience (Digman, 1990; Hogan et al., 1996). Although prior research indicates that the first two traits generally have consistent relationships with job performance (Barrick & Mount, 1991, 2000), they did not predict *normative myopia* in our sample. Nor did emotional stability and openness to experience. Yet agreeableness, or an individual's predilection to be warm and considerate, was highly predictive of *normative myopia* and pay structure preferences. The tendency was for executives who scored low in agreeableness to score high in *normative myopia* and also express a preference for highly differentiated pay. Conversely (and keeping in mind that *myopia* and *receptivity* were reverse-scored), agreeable executives were generally more receptive to factoring values into their decisions and disinclined to favor highly unequal distributions of pay.

Ruling Out Gender?

Conceptually, agreeableness, or an individual's propensity to be warm and considerate, is similar to a gender attribute described in research on ethics of care. Gilligan (1977, 1982), a pioneer in this research, proposed that women place relationships and caring for others at the core of their moral reasoning. Hence, she concluded that Kohlberg's (1981) well-known theory of cognitive moral development, with its apex in justice- and principle-based moral reasoning, does not accurately describe women's moral reasoning. In terms of our study, if men and women differ in moral reasoning, and if agreeableness and caring are similar concepts, then gender must be considered as an explanatory variable. This is especially true because we drew our sample from a highly masculine culture that socializes females to be nurturing, helpful, humble, and affiliating. As such, our female executives might have expressed concern for pay inequities by virtue of their gender, not personality.

To examine this possibility, we analyzed the effect of gender on the self-reported scores of agreeableness *and normative myopia* (both scales ranged from a low score of 1 to a high score of 5). As illustrated in Figure 1.2, we found that the women in our sample were significantly more agreeable than men, which is consistent with previous research in personality psychology (Budaev, 1999; Feingold, 1994). At the same time, our female respondents did not score significantly lower in *normative myopia* than the men. In fact, the two sexes scored similarly on this construct, toward the middle of the range. Moreover, when we statistically controlled for gender, the effect of agreeableness on the dependent variables (*normative myopia* and pay structure preference) increased slightly. We interpreted these combined results to mean that agreeable men are just as likely as agreeable women to exhibit low levels of *normative myopia* and strong preferences for more egalitarian pay structures.

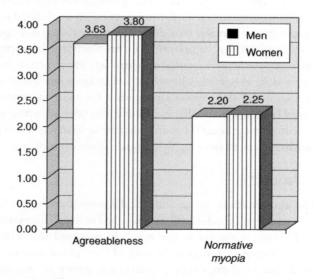

Figure 1.2   Gender differences in agreeableness and *normative myopia*.

The Influence of Business Education

Although personality traits are relatively stable, life experiences can vary significantly to affect individuals' emotions, values, and ethics (Vaidya et al., 2002). Since education is an important life experience, we asked our respondents about their business schooling. Their responses indicated a consistent pattern: those who had taken more business courses scored higher both in *normative myopia* and preference for pay inequalities. This pattern became evident when we separated the respondents into two groups, placing those with more business education in the top 90th percentile (more than 10 courses; $n = 13$) and those with less in the bottom 10 percent (less than 3 courses; $n = 12$).

Figure 1.3 indicates that the means for *normative myopia* and preference for pay differentiation were significantly higher among those executives with maximum exposure to economics, finance, and strategy courses than those with little exposure to these three areas. Based on these statistics, we inferred that courses couched in economics, including finance and strategy, encourage *normative myopia* and preference for exaggerated pay inequalities.

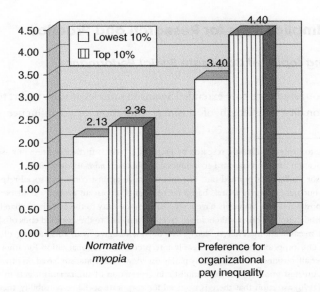

Figure 1.3 Mean values of executives' *normative myopia* and preference for highly differentiated pay systems (by 10th and 90th percentile of amount of business education).

This speculation is consistent with prior theorizing about the effects of business education. For instance, Swanson (1996, 1999) identified two reasons why business education socializes students to resist the idea of corporate social responsibility. One, business education parlays an assumption in standard economics that separates facts from values, relegating the latter to welfare economics and beyond the purview of managerial decision-making (see also Daboub et al., 1995).[2] Two, this theory has been interpreted to glorify narrow self-interest by linking it to the greatest good. The corollary is that there is no need for value awareness among decision-makers, much less value analysis. Perhaps the best-known articulation of this view is Friedman's (1970) proclamation that managers need not be moral agents because their actions are already restrained by standards of public policy, the law, and ethical custom.[3]

We will not fully engage the argument against corporate social responsibility here, except to note that the merits of amoral self-interest have been highly disputed by many scholars (e.g. Frederick, 1986; Sen, 1987; Etzioni, 1988). Besides, the damage inflicted on society by the recent earthquake of corporate scandals should cause even the most ardent supporters of amoral decision-making to rethink their stance.

Some Implications for Research and Practice

Extending Topics of Corporate Social Performance

Based on our study, we have extended Swanson's model of *value neglect* to indicate that personality and length of business education could influence *normative*

---

[2] According to Professor Phillips, research by Frank et al. (1993) further bolsters our assertion that business education based on standard economics contributes to *normative myopia*.

[3] As Professor Phillips has pointed out, Friedman's stance against corporate social responsibility is not amoral but rather overtly moral, based on the rights of private property holders. Specifically, Friedman's position is that managers have a very strict moral duty to the owners or shareholders that preclude consideration of other stakeholders, except as a means to the assumed ends of shareholders (i.e., wealth maximization) (Phillips, 2004). We do not disagree with this reading of Friedman's perspective. Our proposition is that it is easily interpreted as a rationalization for amoral decision-making. After all, business schools typically parlay the view that capitalism based on private property leads to the greatest good. When this simplistic interpretation of utilitarianism gets mixed in with Friedman's (1970) assertion that there is no need for corporate social responsibility, then managers and aspiring managers easily get the message that there is no need for conscious deliberation over values and ethics. Such superficial confounding of economic utilitarianism and Friedman's property rights argument is not surprising, given the lack of ethics coursework in business schools.

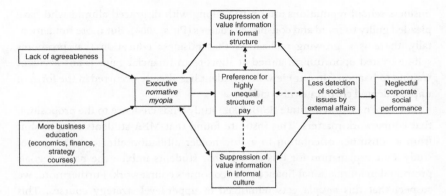

Figure 1.4 Value neglect: a wider context for executive *normative myopia* and neglectful corporate social performance. Adapted from Swanson (1999).

myopia and preference for highly stratified pay. We propose that future business and society research investigate the following propositions, inherent in Figure 1.4.

(1) *Myopic* executives prefer more unequal pay distributions in their organizations. Evidence of this relationship may help predict an organization's tendency to enact *value neglect* or to ignore stakeholder concerns and violate the terms of the social contract between business and society.

  (a) Less agreeable executives tend to be more *myopic* to stakeholder concerns.

  (b) Gender does not predict *normative myopia*.

  (c) Length of business education does help predict *myopia*.

(2) *Receptive* executives prefer more equal pay distributions in their organizations. Evidence of this relationship implies the potential for *value attunement* or an organization's ability to respond constructively to stakeholder concerns and strive to carry out the terms of the social contract between business and society.

  (a) More agreeable executives tend to be more *receptive* to stakeholder concerns.

  (b) Gender does not predict *normative receptivity*.

  (c) Length of business education may offset or decrease *receptivity*.

The last proposition points to the need to rethink business education.

Rethinking Business Education

Calls to rethink business education have grown louder in the wake of the corporate scandals (Adler, 2002; Waddock, 2003; Swanson & Frederick, 2004). For one thing, business school reputations are on trial along with disgraced alumni who have pleaded guilty to fraud and conspiracy charges (Pitts, 2004). But more fundamentally, there is a growing realization that business education that promotes self-interested opportunism aimed at short-term financial gains is an "accident waiting to happen." In our view, the accident has already occurred in the form of unprecedented corporate misconduct.

The Aspen/World Institute (ISIB, 2002) study lends credence to the proposition that coursework matters. This institute found that MBA students tend to shift from a consumer orientation to a stockholder affiliation after only 2 years of study. Our explanation for this shift is that students imbibe the narrow goals promoted in foundational finance and economics coursework. Furthermore, we suspect that this *myopia* gets reinforced in upper-level strategy courses. This dynamic is not necessarily offset by value-based curricula, since only one-third of accredited business schools offer an ethics course (Willen, 2004), and presumably less require one. To make matters worse, many business and society courses that stress the need for corporate social responsibility have been cut from degree programs during the past few years, even in the aftermath of the corporate scandals (Kelly, 2002). This state of affairs is difficult to defend in light of evidence that MBA education may actually cause a decline in moral development (see Jones et al., 1990).

Given that ethics and other behaviorally based skills can be taught and learned (Rest et al., 1999; Rynes et al., 2003), most business schools are missing an opportunity to educate students in their future responsibilities to society. Instead, these schools continue to convey an amoral, even brutish theory of management (Gioia, 2002; Ghoshal, 2003). That students can graduate from business schools with a narrower perspective than they had going in is not lost on the students themselves. Only 22 percent of the MBA students polled said that business schools are doing a lot to prepare them ethically, most adding that they would rather change firms than fight for their own values (ISIB, 2002). This bracketing of personal values, a behavioral artifact of value-free education, stifles the potential for *normative receptivity*. Worse, it may produce the very behaviors assumed in standard economic theory (Pfeffer, 2003).

Given the available evidence, it is easy to make the case that *normative myopia* should be purged from business education. The antidote of infusing values and ethics in curricula would necessitate radical changes in business education over time (Waddock, 2003). Meanwhile, normative education could be enhanced immediately by requiring stand-alone ethics coursework (Swanson & Frederick, 2004).

Revising Criteria for Hiring Executives

Finally, our study has implications for hiring executive managers. Typical screening criteria include personality-organization fit, financial acumen, marketing expertise, and industrial and geographically diverse experiences (Fligstein, 1985; Valentine, 1991; Cappelli, 2000). In terms of the first criterion, hiring for agreeableness might reduce *normative myopia* in top management and help bring about better corporate social performance. Along these lines, hiring executives with personalities befitting existing organizational milieus should be secondary to attracting those capable of using formal and informal mechanisms to bring about *value attunement*. Otherwise, placing myopic executives in charge of organizations that already neglect stakeholder concerns will simply perpetuate the *status quo* and threaten the legitimacy of business as an institution that serves the greater good.

Besides looking for *normative receptivity* in executive candidates, attention should be given to evidence of value-based education, especially since companies headed by finance and administrative CEOs have been found to have higher offending levels of illegal activity than do firms headed by CEOs from other backgrounds (Simpson & Koper, 1997). In terms of our study, this statistic might have something to do with the fact that executives with more economic, finance, and strategy coursework tended to score higher in *normative myopia*. While business schools have been slow in revising curricula to redress this problem, the pace of change might accelerate if hiring practices dictate a demand for executives trained in value awareness and analysis.

Figure 1.4 shows that a preference for highly stratified pay may be a consequence of *normative myopia*. If so, it may by itself predict an executive proclivity to neglect social concerns. We indicate this possibility with two-way broken arrows in Figure 1.4 to stress that more research in this area is needed. Meanwhile, the available evidence suggests that myopic executives are not the best candidates that money can buy, whereas staffing and retaining executives who display *normative receptivity* can be a unique opportunity to improve existing corporate social performance.

Summary

In our study, we found that executives who downplay the importance of values generally prefer to be paid disproportionately large multiples of

> what other employees earn. A striking implication drawn from business and society research is that these same executives will lead their firms in chronically poor corporate social performance. Remedies include educating executives in the importance of value awareness and screening them for *normative myopia* during the hiring process. Given the recent outbreak of corporate misconduct, these issues are highly relevant to business's role in society and warrant further research.

ACKNOWLEDGMENTS

We thank Professors Bob Kolb and Lyla Hamilton and their staff for organizing the *Japha Symposium on The Ethics of Executive Compensation* at which we presented this chapter. We also thank Professor Robert Phillips of the University of San Diego for his constructive comments on our presentation.

REFERENCES

Adler, P. S. 2002. Corporate scandals: it's time for reflection in business schools. *Academy of Management Executive*, **16**(3): 148–149.

Altman, D. 2002. How to tie pay to goals, instead of the stock price. *New York Times*, September 8.

Aspen Initiative for Social Innovation through Business (ISIB) 2002. *Where will they lead? MBA Student Attitudes about Business and Society*. New York: Aspen ISIB.

Austin, J. E. and Kohn, T. O. 1990. *Strategic Management in Developing Countries: Case Studies*. New York: Free Press.

Barrick, M. R. and Mount, M. K. 1991. The big five personality dimensions and job performance: a meta-analysis. *Personnel Psychology*, **44**: 1–26.

Barrick, M. R. and Mount, M. K. 2000. Select on conscientiousness and emotional stability. In E. A. Locke, ed., *The Blackwell Handbook of Principles of Organizational Behavior*. Oxford, UK: Blackwell, pp. 15–28.

Budaev, S. V. 1999. Sex differences in the big five personality factors: testing an evolutionary hypothesis. *Personality and Individual Differences*, **26**: 801–813.

Cappelli, P. 2000. A market-driven approach to retaining talent. *Harvard Business Review*, **78**: 103–111.

Chikudate, N. 2002. Collective myopia and disciplinary power behind the scenes of unethical practices: a diagnostic theory on Japanese organization. *Journal of Management Studies*, **39**: 289–307.

Daboub, A. J., Rasheed, Abdul M. A., Priem, R. L., and Gray, D. A. 1995. Top management team characteristics and corporate illegal activity. *Academy of Management Review*, **20**: 138–170.

Digman, J. M. 1990. Personality structure: emergence of the five-factor model. *Annual Review of Psychology*, **41**: 417–449.

Donaldson, T. 1989. *The Ethics of International Business*. New York: Oxford University Press.

Etzioni, A. 1988. *The Moral Dimension: Toward a New Economics*. New York: Free Press.

Feenstra, R. C. and Hanson, G. 1996. Globalization, outsourcing, and wage inequality. *American Economic Review*, **86**: 240–245.

Feingold, A. 1994. Gender differences in personality: a meta-analysis. *Psychological Bulletin*, **116**: 429–456.

Fligstein, N. 1985. The spread of the multidivisional form among large firms, 1919–1979. *American Sociological Review*, **50**: 377–391.

Frank, R. H., Gilovich, T., and Regan, D. T. 1993. Does studying economics inhibit cooperation? *Journal of Economic Perspectives*, **7**(2): 159–171.

Frederick, W. C. 1986. Toward CSR3: why ethical analysis is indispensable and unavoidable in corporate affairs. *California Management Review*, **28**: 126–141.

Frederick, W. C. 1995. *Values, Nature, and Culture in the American Corporation*. New York: Oxford University Press.

Friedman, M. 1970. The social responsibility of business is to increase its profits. *New York Times Magazine*, **13**: 33, 122–126.

Gilligan, C. 1977. In a different voice: women's conception of the self and of morality. *Harvard Educational Review*, **47**: 481–517.

Gilligan, C. 1982. *In a Different Voice*. Cambridge, MA: Harvard University Press.

Ghoshal, S. 2003. B schools share the blame for Enron: teaching brutal theories leads naturally to management brutality. *Business Ethics*, **4**(Fall).

Gioia, D. A. 2002. Business education's role in the crisis of corporate confidence. *Academy of Management Executive*, **16**: 142–144.

Grossman, W. and Hoskisson, R. E. 1998. CEO pay at the crossroads of Wall Street and main: toward the strategic design of executive compensation. *Academy of Management Executive*, **12**: 43–57.

Hofstede, G. 1980. *Culture's Consequences: International Differences in Work-Related Values*. Beverly Hills, CA: Sage.

Hofstede, G. 2001. *Culture's Consequences: Comparing Values, Behaviors, Institutions, and Organizations across Nations*, 2nd edn. Thousand Oaks, CA: Sage.

Hogan, R., Hogan, J., and Roberts, B. W. 1996. Personality measurement and employment decisions: questions and answers. *American Psychologist*, **51**: 469–477.

Hoppe, M. H. 2004. An interview with Geert Hofstede. *Academy of Management Executive*, **18**: 75–79.

Husted, B. 2000. A contingency theory of corporate social performance. *Business and Society*, **39**: 24–48.

Kelly, M. 2002. It's a heckuva time to be dropping business ethics courses. *Business Ethics*, September/October/November/December: 17–18.

Kohlberg, L. 1981. *Essays in Moral Development: The Philosophy of Moral Development*. New York: Harper & Row.

Jones, T. M., Thomas, T., Agle, B., and Ehreth, J. 1990. Graduate business education and the moral development of MBA students: theory and preliminary research. Paper presented at the annual meeting to the International Association for Business and Society. San Diego, CA.

Logsdon, J. M. and Corzine, J. B. 1999. The CEO's psychological characteristics and ethical culture. *Current Topics in Management*, 4: 63–79.

Murphy, C. 2000. Are the rich cleaning up? *Fortune*, 142: 252–259.

Orlitzky, M. and Swanson, D. L. 2002. Value attunement: toward a theory of socially responsible executive decision making. *Australian Journal of Management*, 27(Special Issue): 119–128.

Pfeffer, J. 2003. Economic logic and language in organization studies: the undermining of critical thinking. Paper presented at the Academy of Management Conference, Seattle, WA.

Phillips, R. 2004. Discussant's comments. Japha Symposium on the Ethics of Executive Compensation. University of Colorado at Boulder.

Pitts, G. 2004. Schools stand trial along with disgraced alumni. *Globe News*, March 8.

Rest, J. R., Narvaez, D., Bebeau, M. J., and Thoma, S. J. 1999. *Postconventional Moral Thinking: A Neo-Kohlbergian Approach*. Mahwah, NJ: Lawrence Erlbaum Associates.

Rynes, S. L. and Gerhart, B. 2000. *Compensation in Organizations: Current Research and Practice*. San Francisco, CA: Jossey-Bass.

Rynes, S. L., Trank, C. Q., Lawson, A. M., and Ilies, R. 2003. Behavioral coursework in business education: growing evidence of a legitimacy crisis. *Academy of Management Learning & Education*, 2: 269–283.

Schein, E. H. 1992. *Organizational Culture and Leadership*, 2nd edn. San Francisco, CA: Jossey-Bass.

Scott, W. G. and Hart, D. K. 1979. *Organizational America*. Boston, MA: Houghton Mifflin.

Sen, A. 1987. *On Ethics and Economics*. Oxford, England: Blackwell.

Sethi, S. P. 1994. *Multinational Corporations and the Impact of Public Advocacy on Corporate Strategy: Nestlé and the Infant Formula Controversy*. Norwell, MA: Kluwer.

Simon, H. 1957. *Administrative Behavior*. New York: Macmillan.

Simpson, S. S. and Koper, C. S. 1997. The changing of the guard: to management characteristics, organizational strain, and antitrust offending. *Journal of Quantitative Criminology*, 13: 373–404.

Swanson, D. L. 1996. Neoclassical economic theory, executive control, and organizational outcomes. *Human Relations*, 49: 735–756.

Swanson, D. L. 1999. Toward an integrative theory of business and society: a research strategy for corporate social performance. *Academy of Management Review*, 24: 506–521.

Swanson, D. L. and Frederick, W. C. 2004. Denial and leadership in business ethics education. In O. C. Ferrell and R. A. Peterson, eds., *Business Ethics: The New Challenge for
Business Schools and Corporate Leader*. New York: M.E. Sharpe.

Thomas, L. Jr. 2004. Day after suit filed over his pay, Grasso comes out fighting. *New York
Times*, May 26.

Triandis, H. C. 2004. The many dimensions of culture. *Academy of Management Executive*,
18: 88–93.

Vaidya, J. G., Gray, E. K., Haig. J., and Watson, D. 2002. On the temporal stability of
personality: evidence for differential stability and the role of life experiences. *Journal of
Personality and Social Psychology*, **83**: 1469–1484.

Valentine, J. A. 1991. A strategy for executive staffing. *Journal of Business Strategy*, **12**: 56–58.

Waddock, S. 2003. A radical agenda for business in society education. Paper presented at
the Academy of Management Conference, Social Issues in Management Division,
Seattle, WA.

Willen, L. 2004. Kellogg denies guilt as B-schools evade alumni lapses. *Bloomberg Press Wire*,
March 8.

2

Does Firm Performance Reduce Managerial Opportunism?

The Impact of Performance-based Compensation and Firm Performance on Illegal Accounting Restatements

Jegoo Lee
Carroll School of Management, Boston College, Chestnut Hill, MA 02467

Byung-Hee Lee
School of Business, Hanyang University, Seoul, Korea, 133-791

Sandra Waddock
Carroll School of Management, Boston College, Chestnut Hill, MA 02467

Samuel B. Graves
Carroll School of Management, Boston College, Chestnut Hill, MA 02467

In this study, we present a timely research with regard to managers' opportunistic behaviors – financial statement manipulation. We inquire as to whether the performance-based compensation (PBC) granted to managers influences managerial opportunism. We further examine whether firm performance reduces managerial opportunism. Specifically, we investigate the moderating roles of firm performance – corporate responsibility (CR) and corporate financial performance (CFP) on managers' opportunistic behaviors. For empirical testing, we used three databases, *KLD* social data, *ExecuComp* data, and *Compustat* data, and employed hierarchical binomial logistic regression analysis. As hypothesized, PBC has a positive and significant effect on managers' opportunistic behaviors,

Parts of this chapter were presented at the annual Academy of Management Conference, New Orleans, LA, 2004. An earlier version of this chapter was presented at the Japha Symposium 2004, Boulder, CO.

measured as accounting restatements. However, better CR does not reduce managers' propensity for accounting restatements; CFP has mixed effects. The study's results suggest the need to develop a deeper understanding of the relationship of firm performance to opportunistic behaviors.

Introduction

Stock options granted to managers have long been touted as a means of resolving agency problems in highly diversified companies, because stock options are granted in an effort to align managers' interests with those of the (diversified) shareholders. Since the Enron scandal broke, however, the public has become well aware that many corporations that awarded huge stock options to top managers *and* engaged in unethical behaviors, such as financial misdealing and irresponsible treatment of shareholders, have simultaneously been touted as paragons of CR. Popular press headlines in the early 2000s broke the expectation that performance-based incentives encourage managers' due diligence, despite some empirical evidence for such alignment (de Bos & Donker, 2004). On the contrary, the scandals raised questions about the effectiveness of stock options as mechanisms for reducing the agency problem.

In numerous recent scandals, some companies' managers were simultaneously creating a good public image for the company aimed at external stakeholders, while internally they were profiteering by disclosing financial results that made the company appear to be doing better financially than it actually was, thus hiding poor performance (Abrahamson & Park, 1994; Vogel, 2001; Gordon, 2002; Tristine, 2003). This type of accounting manipulation is considered to be fraud because it misrepresents the actual financial health of the company. In addition, financial performance has been linked to CR (Margolis & Walsh, 2003; Orlitzky et al., 2003) through the good management hypothesis (Waddock & Graves, 1997a), so it might also be assumed that a financially excellent company is also a good corporate citizen.

The experience of the past few years suggests that managers who are granted stock options could easily be seduced into manipulating the company's apparent financial results by manipulating financial and accounting statements (*Business Week*, 1998; *Interactive Week*, 2001; Ketz, 2003a,b). These very companies may well be considered among the "most admired" because of their presumed financial performance, as was Enron for many years prior to its debacle. According to these cases, because accounting restatements frequently reflect internal ethical issues, the existence of accounting restatements provides a research site to explore the inappropriate opportunism of managers who have been granted stock options.

In this study, we examine the effect of stock options as PBC on managers' manipulation of financial statements, which are used as evidence of inappropriate internal practices (Merchant & Rockness, 1994; Grant et al., 2000; Elias, 2002). In addition, we also examine the impact of firm performance on the effect of stock options – whether good or bad performance of the firm influences the internal mechanisms that underlie (ir)responsible behaviors in companies. This chapter is constituted as follows. In the next section, we develop a theoretical framework for exploring the links discussed above. Following the literature review, we introduce the research model with the main variables: PBC, earnings management (accounting restatements), CR, and CFP. Then, we discuss the datasets and research methodology – hierarchical binomial logistic regression – used to analyze the data. Finally, we will lay out the findings and implications of this study.

Literature Review

To examine the effect of PBC and the influence of firm performance, we review several theoretical viewpoints and concepts. First, we briefly summarize the background of PBC, that is, stock options. Second, as an indicator of managers' opportunistic behavior, earnings management is introduced. Then, two theoretical constructs with regard to firm performance, CR and CFP, which could conceivably neutralize opportunism or encourage due diligence of managers who are granted PBC, are introduced.

Performance-based Compensation (Stock Options)

Performance-based Compensation encourages managers to produce good performance and be rewarded accordingly (Sanders, 2001; Certo et al., 2003). It was originally intended to improve managers' due diligence with respect to firm performance, and includes as its primary mechanism the granting of stock options. As a result, the performance-based incentive binds managers' interests to shareholders' benefits because managers who are given PBC will share the *same* performance goals as shareholders (for an extensive discussion on the effect of performance-based or outcome-based compensation, see Eisenhardt, 1988, 1989).

According to agency theory, managers' self-interest may conflict with the interest of owners or shareholders for wealth maximization (Eisenhardt, 1988, 1989; Kim, 2002). Due to information asymmetry, however, managers have more insight into the company's performance and problems than do shareholders or owners, who thus need a monitoring system to govern managers' behaviors (Kaufman et al., 1995; St-Onge et al., 2001). PBC or outcome-based incentives are meant to resolve the agency problem by aligning executives' interests with those of shareholders, explicitly by making managers into owners. Thus, from the shareholders' viewpoint, PBC is granted for the purpose of producing high financial returns.

From the managers' perspectives, there must be powerful incentives from PBC to achieve high levels of financial performance, because these results will ultimately provide high personal compensation to the manager as well (Bass et al., 1997). In principle, the higher the stock value is, the more benefit managers will be granted via their stock options, and the more they will be in-line with shareholder objectives of maximizing financial benefits (Daily et al., 2003). Under a PBC system, agency problems between managers and shareholders are resolved in theory.

A serious question regarding the effectiveness of PBC remains: does PBC actually resolve the problem of opportunistic behaviors by managers, that is, is the agency problem settled by such compensation schemes? A relevant but urgent issue is not whether a manager will be loyal to shareholders' interests, but to which kind of shareholders' interests. In general, shareholders' interests focus exclusively on financial performance, for example, return on assets (ROA), return on equity (ROE), or returns on sales (ROS) (for reviews, see Pava & Krausz, 1996; Roman et al., 1999; Margolis & Walsh, 2003; Orlitzky et al., 2003). Based on shareholders' interest in high financial performance, managers who are granted PBCs are supposed to pursue high financial performance.

Unfortunately, scholars have largely ignored the issue of managers' strategic responses to stock or equity ownership (Sanders, 2001), which suggests the need to explore how managers actually behave to generate high financial performance. Whether managers do respond diligently to shareholders' desires is important, because beyond the evidence of numerous scandals in which shareholders were greatly harmed, there is some, albeit inconsistent, empirical evidence that managers do not always blindly follow shareholders' performance expectations (Daily et al., 2003). There have been some research findings that provide clues for this suspicion. There is no clear linkage between managers' level of equity ownership and firm performance (Daily et al., 2003). More specifically, under different environmental conditions, such as stock-market stability and regulatory reform, PBC affects managerial behaviors differently (Kim, 2002; Welch, 2002). In addition, under certain circumstances, however, it appears that PBC functions as a catalyst that can lead managers to manipulate financial reports or performance (Sanders, 2001; Welch, 2002).

This line of thinking suggests that it is necessary to inquire more deeply into the effects of PBC on managers' behavior, particularly as it relates to accounting manipulations. To examine the effectiveness of PBC, this study focuses attention on earnings management as a managerial behavior intended to produce the appearance of better financial performance than actually exists.

Earnings Management (Accounting Restatements)

Manipulation of earnings (accounting restatements or earnings management) can be said to represent the extent to which managers are willing to place achieving (apparent) superior financial performance above reporting actual results. More specifically, earnings management at the division level is "a division manager's actions to serve to increase (or decrease) current reported earnings of the division without a corresponding increase (or decrease) in the long-term economic profitability of this division" (Fischer & Rosenzweig, 1995). Applied at the corporate level, earnings management is intended to boost stock prices, thereby increasing the returns to shareholders – including executives who have been granted stock options (Demski et al., 1984).

Earnings management occurs (1) when managers alter financial reporting either to mislead some stakeholders or to influence contractual outcomes depending on accounting numbers (Healy & Wahlen, 1999) and (2) when financial manipulations are used to produce desirable earnings figures, irrespective of a company's actual financial performance – in what are called "aggressive accounting practices" (GAO, 2002). In spite of the rigorous guidelines of Generally Accepted Accounting Principles (GAAP), some managers fabricate a certain portion of the earnings – so-called non-GAAP *pro forma* earnings – out of their own desires to achieve future performance results (Ketz, 2003a,b).

Stakeholders outside the firms are generally unaware of earnings management until the company restates its accounting reports (Burns, 2003; Richardson et al., 2003), indicating that earnings have been (deliberately) misreported. Before an accounting restatement, outsiders can hardly be expected to recognize managers' unethical manipulation of financial performance. The critical point is that earnings management veils the genuine outcomes of managerial behaviors and corporate performance. According to former Securities and Exchange Commission (SEC) Chairman Arthur Levitt, Jr, "[T]he overall consequence of earnings management is the erosion of trust between shareholders and companies" (Levitt, 1998; cited in Elias, 2002).

From the economic point of view, the resulting costs can be tragically high. According to Huron Consulting Group (2003), the number of companies undertaking accounting restatements, which reflect varying degrees of earnings management and accounting manipulation, rose from 270 in 2001 to 330 in 2002, a 22 percent increase. What is worse is that shareholders, the purported priority stakeholders, were the victims of these unethical manipulations by managers. For instance, in the high-tech industry, accounting restatements by 30 companies brought about losses of some $73 billion to shareholders (*Business Week*, 1998; *Interactive Week*, 2001).

Therefore, earnings management reflects negative due diligence of managers in their fiduciary duty to shareholders (for extensive discussion of unethical properties of earnings management, see Merchant & Rockness, 1994; Kaplan, 2001; Elias, 2002). Beyond the financial issues, earnings management represents managers' irresponsible behavior with respect to outside stakeholders, especially investors. Manipulating accounting statement represents socially undesirable behavior as well as illegal activities.

What is the impact of PBC on managers' earnings management? We can propose two contrasting relationships. First, based on the original assumptions about stock options programs, managers who are granted PBC should manage their companies with considerable due diligence. PBC is proposed as a resolution to tensions arising between shareholders' benefits and managers' interests, or what has been called the agency problem (Jensen & Meckling, 1976; Fama, 1980).

When managers receive PBC, they may have little incentive to manage earnings because they attempt to establish transparency with respect to outside stakeholders. The rationale is that a manager is responsive not only by compensation but also by due diligence to investors. Furthermore, if they are actually operating in good faith, they would not need to hide their poor financial achievement. A corresponding hypothesis is,

Hypothesis 1a: PBC is negatively associated with earnings management (or accounting restatement).

Second, when granted PBC, a manager's bonus is typically tied to meeting certain financial targets, which in theory motivate managers to engage in earnings management in an effort to maximize their bonus. This latter effect has been termed the bonus maximization hypothesis (Gaver et al., 1995; Holthausen et al., 1995; Guidry et al., 1999). When managers perceive goals to be within reach, they have incentives to actively pursue the goals, even if through unethical means (Guidry et al., 1999; Schweitzer et al., 2002). Some previous research results demonstrate the positive relationships between PBC and earnings management, both unethical behavior and negative enactment of fiduciary duty (Baker et al., 2002; Lee, 2002; Kedia, 2003; Richardson et al., 2003). In principle, these studies indicate that earnings management is more likely to happen when managers are motivated by PBC than when they are rewarded through other means.

For the reasons mentioned above, when managers receive PBC, they may well be stimulated to manage earnings (cf. Bass et al., 1997; Johnson & Greening, 1999). A corresponding hypothesis is,

> *Hypothesis 1b:* PBC is positively associated with earnings management (or accounting restatement).

In addition, we will examine the effect of the firm performance that may influence the managers' motivation to manipulate or not to manipulate financial statements. We will review two factors with the relevant theoretical rationales below.

Firm Performance

Several research results have pointed out the influence of contextual factors on the way stock options granted to managers affect their decision-making (Amburgey & Miner, 1992; Westphal & Zajac, 1994). In this study, we will employ two conceptualizations of firm performance: CR and CFP.

Corporate Responsibility

Corporate responsibility (CR) represents the ways in which a company exhibits its responsibilities to the multiple primary and secondary stakeholders that enable it to exist within society through its operating practices (Clarkson, 1995; Waddock, 2000). For several decades, scholars have examined the relationships between CR and firm performance (see Pava and Krausz, 1996; Margolis & Walsh, 2003; Orlitzky et al., 2003 for extensive surveys of the literature). Overall, the results indicate either neutral or slightly positive relationships.

The positive correlation between CR performance and financial performance suggests that CR and financial performance are compatible. The simple rationale is that attention to CR improves relationships with key stakeholders, resulting in better overall performance (Waddock & Graves, 1997a; Hillman & Keim, 2001; Orlitzky et al., 2003). Positive perceptions from outside stakeholders should lead to increased sales and cost reduction to stakeholders (McGuire et al., 1988, 1990). Likewise, good financial achievement turns out to benefit companies, as they may be in a position to invest in activities with regard to corporate *social* performance (Carroll, 1998). Therefore, CR reflects the quality of managerial decision-making, and there should be a relationship between CR and managerial behavior (Swanson, 1995, 1999; Waddock & Graves, 1997b).

Under the conditions of strong CR, individual managers should be encouraged to keep their due diligence, or they may not as easily be able to pursue only their personal objectives related to financial returns. With the presence of PBC granted to managers, there is some chance that managers will undertake a more honest approach to accounting for results when strong company norms of responsible practice support their due diligence. This moderating effect of CR suggests that the desirable effect of PBC may be reinforced depending on the company's level of CR.

From the bonus maximization perspective, although PBC may provoke managers to manipulate financial achievements to seek their own interests, strong CR could lessen this effect, and might galvanize managers to be more fiscally responsible and act with greater due diligence. Based on this view, when managers are given PBC, for example, stock options, there is some possibility that these incentives will refocus managerial attention on achieving good financial bottom-line results by whatever means are available, including earnings manipulations that require eventual accounting restatements so that they can line their own pockets.

In both circumstances, managers' incentives to manipulate company earnings could be reduced. A corresponding hypothesis is:

> *Hypothesis 2:* CR negatively moderates the positive (negative) relationship between PBC and accounting restatement.

Corporate Financial Performance

Actual corporate financial performance (CFP) may also moderate the effect of PBC on manipulation of financial earnings for two reasons. First, with good financial achievement, managers do not have much incentive to manipulate their financial statements. Second, there could be a positive relationship between good CFP and managers' due diligence in dealing with stakeholders (Waddock & Graves, 1997a;

Sanders, 2001; Margolis & Walsh, 2003). From this perspective, CFP is an input for preventing inappropriate earnings management.

Managers' due diligence is a key to managers' responsibilities to stakeholders, especially shareholders. Thus, the thinking goes that if a company's financial performance is positive, its managers' due diligence will be strengthened. In other words, CFP reflects managers' due diligence, because it implies responsibility to shareholders (Hillman & Keim, 2001). In a responsibility framework, decision-making managers who achieve good financial performance should not have any reason to misbehave (Agle et al., 1999; Weaver et al., 1999a,b). Previous research has also found that companies with good performance are more likely to produce social disclosure through company reports (Ullman, 1985; Gelb & Strawser, 2001). In short, when companies already have excellent financial performance, they have little reason to manipulate their financial achievements.

In brief, good CFP is expected to reduce agency problems between managers and shareholders. On the other hand, when managers are granted extensive PBC, for example, in the form of stock options, there is some possibility that they pay greater attention to reaching financial bottomline results by whatever means are available, including earnings manipulations that require eventual accounting restatements. In this sense, we can build a proposition that with excellent firm performance managers tend to frame the situation positively and are likely to maintain the *status quo* reporting strategy of no manipulation. Thus:

> *Hypothesis 3:* CFP negatively moderates the positive (negative) relationship between PBC and accounting restatements.

In Figure 2.1, the independent variable, PBC is expected to be negatively (Hypothesis 1a) or positively (Hypothesis 1b) associated with more accounting

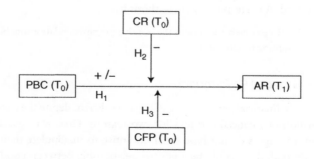

Figure 2.1   Research model.

restatements, the dependent variable. Both CR and CFP are expected to have negative moderating roles on the relationship between the independent and dependent variables. Based on our hypotheses and model, both firm performance are expected to strengthen managers' due diligence or to weaken their opportunistic behaviors, when they are given PBC.

Methods

Sample

Restatements resulting from inaccurate reporting of financial statements lose investors' confidence and undermine fair valuation activity of the stock market. As a result, earnings restatements are used in the present study as an indicator of poor managerial fiduciary duty to shareholders. To obtain data on a firm's fiduciary duty, we relied on a report on financial restatements published in 2002 by the US General Accounting Office (GAO, 2002). The GAO report collected 919 cases of financial restatement announcements made by 845 public firms from January 1, 1997 to June 30, 2002. The cases involved instances in which firms corrected their previously released financial statements caused by material errors and fraud[1] so that the restatement cases tended to reflect firm behaviors detrimental to shareholder value. The GAO report enhanced its accuracy and completeness by comparing its cases with those compiled by SEC, the Congressional Research Service, and others when information was available. Our study reduced sampling bias that may be potentially caused by subjective and proprietary data collection process by using publicly available and accurate GAO data. For the sample, we selected restatement cases announced from January 2001 to June 2002, when the issue of accounting fraud caught the attention of the public following the Enron scandal in 2000.

The sample consists of firms included in a database compiled by Kinder, Lydenberg, and Domini (KLD).[2] The KLD database has been used in other studies on CR (e.g., Waddock & Graves, 1997a; Johnson & Greening, 1999) and is recognized as one of the most comprehensive multidimensional databases. The database includes all of the S&P 500, large cap firms in the United States.

---

[1] The restatement cases in the GAO report did not include announcements involving stock splits, changes in accounting principles, and other financial restatements that were not made to correct mistakes in the application of accounting standards.

[2] For detailed descriptions on the KLD database, refer to Waddock and Graves (1997a,b).

Following the study of Richardson et al. (2003) which reported an average of 1.8 years time lapse between the end of the fiscal year of alleged manipulation and the announcement of the restatement, we used compensation and financial data filed for 1999, 2 years prior to the sample restatement announcements to obtain company sample. Of the 663 firms in the 1999 *KLD* dataset, 52 firms were identified as having engaged in restatement activity during the relevant period. Compensation and financial data were drawn from Standard and Poor's *ExecuComp* database and *Compustat*. After excluding cases for which CR and compensation data were not available, the sample size reduced from 663 to 585 in total, with 43 firms remaining in the restatement category. The sample size was reduced once more, due to missing data for several other control variables. As a result, the final sample size in this study is 400, among them 32 companies restated their financial earnings and accounting statements.

Measures

We used three main variables, accounting restatement, PBC, and CFP with control variables. We employed four datasets, the GAO restatement report (2002) for a yes/no assessment of earnings restatements, the *KLD* database for the CR data, and the *ExecuComp* and *Compustat* databases for financial performance data. Below we outline the process of building measures.

Dependent Variable: Accounting Restatement

The dependent variable for all hypothesis testing was accounting restatement, the result of earnings managements. Accounting restatement typically results from managers' manipulation of companies' earnings for several years, and demonstrates the extent of managers' manipulation to their investors when made public. Thus, we used a firm's restatement announcement as a proxy for its earnings management. A restatement can be coded as a binary variable: a firm that announced a restatement is coded as 1, while a firm with a no-restatement record is coded as 0.

Independent Variable: PBC

To measure PBC as an independent variable, we collected compensation data for all currently appointed executives and not just CEOs, because many companies involved in the accounting scandals, such as Enron and Tyco, revealed that a group of executives other than the CEO were involved.[3] PBC was measured as the fraction of total compensation. PBC is the sum of the value of the current-year stock options grants derived from the Black–Scholes method and the market value of restricted stocks granted during the fiscal year. All compensation data were drawn from S&P's *ExecuComp* database.

Moderating Variable: CR

Corporate responsibility is an elusive construct to measure (Clarkson, 1995). For this research, we used the *KLD* database because one of its advantages is that the database includes multiple firm attributes to measure CR. Five of the rated attributes have usually been used in other studies (e.g., Johnson & Greening, 1999). These attributes are community relations, employee relations, firm performance with regard to the natural environment, treatment of women and minority, and product characteristics. We used two more attributes – non-US operations and governance-related issues, as well as negative screens such as alcoholic concerns, gambling concerns, tobacco concerns, firearms concerns, military concerns, and nuclear concerns.

Since the number of firms included in the database and the distribution of CR scores varies across industries (Waddock & Graves, 1997a,b), we controlled for industry variations by centering firms' CR scores with each industry mean. Following Waddock and Graves (1997a), Table 2.1 presents a list of 14 industries, number of firms in each industry categorized by SIC codes, and average industry CR scores. The sum of mean-centered CR scores on the five attributes was used to represent each firm's CR.

Moderating Variable: CFP

As reviewed earlier, prior research has indicated that financial and firm characteristic variables may be associated with restatements (Kedia, 2003; Richardson et al., 2003). In particular, we include three moderating variables regarding financial performance, ROA, ROE, and ROS. These measures were drawn from the *Compustat* database.

---

[3] Section 302 of the Sarbanes-Oxley Act (2002) requiring CEO and CFO certification of quarterly financial statements also points to the collective behaviors of executives in accounting manipulation.

Table 2.1   Industries in the sample

Industry	SIC	N	CR	Min.	Max.
Mining, construction	100–1999	27	4.22	0	11
Food, textile, apparel	2000–2390	38	3.92	0	10
Forest products, paper, publishing	2391–2780	48	3.63	0	11
Chemicals, pharmaceuticals	2781–2890	44	6.02	0	20
Refining, rubber, plastic	2891–3199	19	6.47	1	17
Containers, steel, heavy manufacturing	3200–3569	46	3.54	0	10
Computers, autos, aerospace	3570–3990	99	4.82	0	15
Transportation	3991–4731	17	3.88	1	9
Telephone, utilities	4732–4991	67	4.15	0	13
Wholesale, retail	4992–5990	66	2.80	0	9
Bank, financial services	6150–6700	81	4.22	0	14
Hotel, entertainment	6800–8051	40	3.53	0	15
Hospital management	8052–8744	7	3.00	2	5
Industrial conglomerate	9900–9997	3	8.33	5	14

In addition, we also included several control variables in this study: 3-year annual growth rate of earnings per share, firm size (log of total assets), and the number of employees.

To determine the causal relationships among independent variables and the dependent variable, we used a time lag in the model. Earnings management is measured by restatements of the firm, because restatements in the present (T_1) reflect earnings management in previous years (T_0). According to previous research results, high CR in previous years (T_0) leads to financial performance in the present (T_1), and high CFP in previous years (T_0) leads to managerial due diligence in the present (T_1). PBC given in previous years (T_0) influences managerial behavior in the present (T_1), because PBC can be realized after a certain amount of time has passed, thus a 2-year lag was used. (In our study, T_0 means 1999 and T_1 means 2001–2002.)

Analysis

Hierarchical binomial logistic regression analysis was conducted for the estimation of all models. There are two reasons why we use this statistical technique. First, the dependent variable, accounting restatement, is a categorical variable – whether earnings management has been conducted or not, that is, the 0/1 coding for earning restatements. Second, we can check the significance of each variable, and change in variance explained as each variable, is added in the model. Within this procedure, the control variables were entered first, the direct effect variable was entered second, and then the moderating effects were added. Lastly, a full model with all of the variables including the interaction term was estimated.

Results

Table 2.2 provides the descriptive statistics, including means, standard deviations, and correlations, of the variables used in the study. First, we note that all of the financial performance variables are significantly and positively correlated with each other. Significant and negative correlations exist between CR measures from the *KLD* database and total assets, suggesting that larger firms generally exhibit less positive stakeholder-related practices. Interestingly, larger firms are more negatively correlated with CFP, such as ROA and ROS, than are relatively smaller ones. None of the variables is significantly associated with accounting restatements, and only ROA exhibits a positive relationship with CR.

Tests of Hypotheses

In the first step of hierarchical logistic regression, we included only control variables and an independent variable in order to test Hypotheses 1a and 1b. Hypothesis 1a predicted that PBC is negatively associated with accounting restatements; while Hypothesis 1b predicted a positive association between them. As shown in the model 1 column in Table 2.3, no control variable has a significant coefficient. However, the independent variable, PBC, has a positive and significant coefficient, as Hypothesis 1b predicted. Therefore, Hypothesis 1a is not supported, but Hypothesis 1b is.

In model 2, we tested both Hypothesis 1 and Hypothesis 2. Hypothesis 2 predicted that CR will negatively moderate the effect of PBC on accounting restatement. As hypothesized, we found a positive association of the moderating effect from CR to the relationship between PBC and accounting restatement, but the effect is not statistically significant. Thus, Hypothesis 2 is not supported. Moreover, the increase in χ^2 from model 1 with control variables to model 2 with two independent variables is not significant.

Table 2.2 Means, standard deviations, and correlations[a]

Variable	Mean	s.d.	1	2	3	4	5	6	7	8	9	10	11	12
1. Restatement (Yes = 1)	0.08	0.27												
2. PBC	0.46	0.24	0.07											
3. CR	0.06	2.59	0.07	0.01										
4. ROAs	6.84	6.01	−0.03	0.07	0.10*									
5. ROE	20.00	22.95	0.07	0.02	0.01	0.56**								
6. Return on sales	0.09	0.08	−0.09	0.14**	0.07	0.56**	0.35**							
7. Interaction (2 × 3)	0.07	1.58	0.11	0.10*	0.90**	−0.05	0.01	−0.04						
8. Interaction (2 × 4)	3.22	4.15	0.01	0.50**	0.05	0.78**	0.37**	0.55**	−0.02					
9. Interaction (2 × 5)	9.25	11.87	0.10	0.42**	0.01	0.50*	0.82**	0.40**	0.05	0.64**				
10. Interaction (2 × 6)	0.04	0.06	−0.04	0.51**	0.03	0.46**	0.24**	0.84**	0.05	0.74**	0.53**			
11. Assets[b]	3.79	0.72	−0.03	0.22**	−0.14**	−0.36**	−0.04	0.15*	0.39**	−0.15	0.07	0.17**		
12. Employee number	42.10	86.60	0.01	0.07	−0.02	−0.03	0.01	−0.12*	0.30**	0.00	0.04	−0.06	0.32**	
13. 3-year growth rate of earnings per share	15.50	47.13	−0.05	0.11*	0.07	0.27**	0.18**	0.18**	−0.05	0.27**	0.20**	0.18**	−0.08	−0.05

Notes: *p < .05, **p < .01

[a] n = 400; [b]Logarithm.

Table 2.3   Results of hierarchical logistic regression analysis[a]

Variable	Model 1	Model 2	Model 3	Model 4	Hypothesis
Constant	$-1.95^{\dagger}$	$-1.97^{\dagger}$	-2.64^{*}	-2.93^{*}	
Controls					
Assets[b]	-0.31	-0.30	-0.12	-0.03	
Employee number	0.00	0.00	0.00	0.00	
3-year growth rate of earnings per share	-0.01	-0.01	-0.01	-0.01	
Direct effects					
PBC	$1.44^{\dagger}$	$1.50^{\dagger}$	$1.85^{\dagger}$	$1.83^{\dagger}$	H1a/H1b
CR		-0.17		-0.14	
ROA			-0.01	-0.02	
ROE			-1.31	-1.36	
ROS			10.31	7.64	
Interaction effects					
PBC × CR		0.20		0.22	H2
PBC × ROA			0.02	0.02	H3
PBC × ROE			$0.03^{\dagger}$	$0.03^{\dagger}$	H3
PBC × ROS			$-13.49^{\dagger}$	$-15.90^{\dagger}$	H3
χ^2	5.26	5.31	11.00	13.63^{*}	
d.f.	4	5	7	8	
$\Delta\chi^2$		0.05	5.74^{*}	8.37^{*}	
-2 Log likelihood	218.42	218.37	207.10	204.46	
Cox and Snell R^2	0.01	0.02	0.03	0.03	

Notes: $^{\dagger}p < .10$; $^{*}p < .05$.

[a] $n = 400$; [b] Logarithm.

Model 3 in Table 2.3 tests Hypothesis 1a, Hypothesis 1b, and Hypothesis 3, predicting that CFP negatively moderates the relationship between PBC and accounting restatements. A statistically significant and negative interaction was found for ROS (PBC × ROS). In addition, the interaction effect for ROE (PBC × ROE) was statistically significant, but the direction was contrary to that hypothesized, a positive effect. No significant effect was found for ROA (PBC × ROA). The results partially support the interaction effect postulated in Hypothesis 3. In addition, compared to model 1 and model 2, the increase in χ^2 is significant ($p < .05$).

Model 4 is the complete model, which includes all independent and moderating variables, to test all four hypotheses. As shown in Table 2.3, there is a direct effect between PBC and its interaction effect with ROE, as both have positive and significant coefficients, implying that these two effects positively predict accounting restatements or earnings management. Only one moderating effect, the interaction effect of PBC and ROS, has a negative and significant coefficient, implying that ROS reduces the positive relationships between PBC and accounting restatements. CR, however, shows no interaction effect with PBC. In addition, the increase in χ^2 is significant, compared with any of the previous models ($p < .05$).

In short, a hypothesis, namely H1b, for bonus maximization, which implies that PBC would be positively related to accounting restatements or earnings management, was fully supported. The findings for Hypothesis 2, namely that CR would weaken managers' opportunistic behaviors, were not significant but the directionality was as hypothesized (model 2). Hypothesis 3, which implies that CFP would moderate the relationship between PBC and accounting restatement, was partly supported (model 3). Moreover, results for Hypotheses 2 and 3 provide controversial results (model 4).

Discussion

In this study, we attempted to figure out the effects of PBC on managers' opportunism using unethical financial manipulations as a measure. This topic was, as mentioned, ignited by the corporate scandals that have made headlines in the early part of the new millennium. As hypothesized, PBC has a positive impact on earnings management. Although this result is expected, it implies that the agency problem between managers and shareholders is not resolved by PBC.

Indeed, the outcome presented above is the reverse of the traditional agency theory prediction and indicates that PBC, in this case, stock options, is far from a panacea for agency problems and may even create incentives for managerial opportunistic behaviors that are clearly unethical. These financial manipulations hurt the shareholder, who is the intended beneficiary of aligning executive compensation with financial performance, under traditional financial theory as well as agency theory. Thus, the currently prevalent practice of linking executive compensation to company performance may create unintended ethical and accounting problems when performance is directly linked to compensation.

Further, two more issues are uncovered in this study. First, CR is not necessarily a stable predictor of responsible managerial behavior. After the exposure of several corporate icons, who were previously thought to exhibit highly responsible behavior as having serious accounting misrepresentation (e.g., Enron), overt expressions of CR have become somewhat controversial in the eyes of critical observers (e.g., Entine, 2003). The cynicism of critics arises because business firms committed illegal or socially undesirable practices even though they apparently managed their stakeholder responsibilities well (e.g., Derber, 1998). Rather than CR being fully institutionalized or actually internalized as exhibiting the values-in-practice within a company, our findings indicate that CR is dealt with as an exogenous factor that yields a positive image for the company. It may simply take some time for managers to fully adapt and internalize corporate social responsible practices, or any other new practices, into their companies (Mintzberg, 1981; Waddock & Graves, 1997b), as much as 20 years as Gibson and Tesone's (2001) research on management fads indicates.

Second, CFP does not consistently predict the likelihood of earnings management. In particular, we found opposing roles of ROE and ROS, with undesirable and desirable results, respectively. ROE reinforces the positive relationships between PBC and accounting restatement; meanwhile, ROS reduces the effect of PBC on managers' earnings manipulations. Although both ROE and ROS are representative proxies for financial performance of firms, their functions in this study are contrary to each other. A possible reason is that the denominators, equity and sales, are not same. Equity is the difference between assets and liability; thus, the ROE value is positively proportional with liability and far more sensitive to debt or the amount of financial risk that a company has undertaken. We can conjecture that companies with high liabilities are more likely to manipulate their financial statements than companies with lower liabilities because the ROE measure is one which investors are quite concerned about. With regard to ROS, companies with higher sales are more likely to conduct earnings management than companies with smaller sales. Thus, size matters.

Limitations

Two shortcomings of this study should be mentioned. First, it would be interesting to reproduce the study using added variables on corporate governance, especially on managers' compensation. For example, managers' equity ownership may have different effects than managers' stock options. In addition, we tested the hypotheses only using OLS regression models, but there may be nonlinear effects that would show up using other models. We might also hypothesize that there are curvilinear effects of PBC on managers' due diligence in implementing their fiduciary duties.

Second, we only employed datasets for one time period, T_0, 1999 and T_1, 2001–2002; however, it would be interesting to expand the study to test additional time periods as well as different lags. Moreover, a specific environmental situation would have an effect on managers' earnings management. For instance, under conditions of stock-market volatility, financial ownership undermines psychological ownership, because having stock options during a bull market provides managers with an unstable sense of security (Welch, 2002). Although accounting restatement happens at a specific point in time, earnings management is a process that presumably occurs over a longer time period and may last several years. Thus, it is important to examine the effects of PBC, CR, and CFP over several years.

Implications for Future Research

An interesting implication from this study is that the agency theory's propositions about aligning executive compensation with performance may be misguided. PBC is apparently associated with less fiduciary responsibility. Moreover, regardless of corporate performance, managers' self-interest cannot be controlled even under their purported primary (sole) "objective function" (e.g., Jensen, 2001). It is clear that we still do not fully understand how managers implement their own self-interest, but it does appear that managers' self-centered perspectives can sometimes override their due diligence and fiduciary responsibilities even to shareholders, not to mention their responsibilities to other stakeholders. Few other issues are more urgent than the need to learn to design organizational incentives so that executives' incentives are aligned with their actual duties – to shareholders and to the vast array of other stakeholders who also make investments in the business.

REFERENCES

Abrahamson, E. and Park, C. 1994. Concealment of negative organization outcomes: an agency theory perspective. *Academy of Management Journal*, 37(5): 1302–1334.

Agle, B. R., Mitchell, R. K., and Sonnenfeld, J. A. 1999. Who matters to CEOs? An investigation of stakeholder attributes and salience, corporate performance and CEO values. *Academy of Management Journal*, 42(5): 507–525.

Amburgey, T. L. and Miner, A. S. 1992. Strategic momentum: the effects of repetitive, positional, and contextual momentum on merger activity. *Strategic Management Journal*, 13(5): 335–348.

Baker, T., Collins, D., and Reitenga, A. 2002. Stock option compensation and earnings management incentives. Working paper, University of Houston, Houston, TX.

Bass, K. E., Simerly, R. L., and Li, M. 1997. The effects of CEO compensation on corporate economic performance and corporate social performance. *Academy of Management Proceedings*. Boston, MA.

Burns, N. 2003. Does performance-based incentives explain restatements? Ph.D. Dissertation, Ohio State University.

Carroll, A. 1998. The four faces of corporate citizenship. *Business and Society Review: Journal of the Center for Business Ethics at Bentley College*, **100/101**: 1–7.

Certo, S. T., Daily, C. M., Cannella, A. A., and Dalton, D. R. 2003. Giving money to get money: how CEO stock options and CEO equity enhance IPO evaluations. *Academy of Management Journal*, **46**(5): 643–653.

Clarkson, M. E. 1995. A stakeholder framework for analyzing and evaluating corporate social performance. *Academy of Management Review*, **20**(1): 92–117.

Daily, C. M., Dalton, D. R., and Rajagopalan, N. 2003. Governance through ownership: centuries of practice, decades of research. *Academy of Management Journal*, **46**(2): 151–158.

de Bos, A. and Donker, H. 2004. Monitoring accounting changes: empirical evidence from the Netherlands. *Corporate Governance*, **12**(1): 60–73.

Demski, J., Patell, J., and Wolson, M. 1984. Decentralized choice of monitoring systems. *The Accounting Review*, **59**: 16–34.

Derber, C. 1998. *Corporation Nation: How Corporations Are Taking Over Our Lives and What We Can Do About It*. New York: St Martin's Press.

Eisenhardt, K. M. 1988. Agency- and institutional-theory explanations: the case of retail sales compensation. *Academy of Management Journal*, **31**(3): 488–511.

Eisenhardt, K. M. 1989. Agency theory: an assessment and review. *Academy of Management Review*, **14**(1): 57–74.

Elias, R. Z. 2002. Determinants of earnings management ethics among accountants. *Journal of Business Ethics*, **40**: 33–45.

Entine, J. 2003. The myth of social investing: a critique of its practice and consequences for corporate social performance research. *Organization and Environment*, **16**(3): 352–368.

Fama, E. 1980. Agency problems and the theory of the firm. *Journal of Political Economy*, **88**: 288–307.

Fischer, M. and Rosenzweig, K. 1995. Attitudes of students and accounting practitioners concerning the ethical acceptability of earnings management. *Journal of Business Ethics*, **14**(6): 433–444.

Gaver, J., Gaver, K., and Austin, J. 1995. Additional evidence on bonus plan and income management. *Journal of Accounting and Economics*, **18**: 3–28.

Gelb, D. S. and Strawser, J. A. 2001. Corporate social responsibility and financial disclosures: an alternative explanation for increased disclosure. *Journal of Business Ethics*, **33**: 1–13.

Gibson, J. W. and Tesone, D. V. 2001. Management fads: emergence, evolution, and implications for managers. *Academy of Management Executive*, **15**(4): 122–133.

Gordon, J. N. 2002. What Enron means for the management and control of the modern corporation: some initial reflections. *University of Chicago Law Review*, **69**(3): 1233–1251.

Grant, C. T., Depree, M., Chauncey, M., and Grant, G. H. 2000. Earnings management and the abuse of materiality. *Journal of Accountancy*, **190**: 41–44.

Guidry, F., Leone, A. J., and Rock, S. 1999. Earnings-based bonus plans and earnings management by business-unit managers. *Journal of Accounting and Economics*, **26**: 113–142.

Healy, P. M. and Wahlen, J. M. 1999. A review of the earnings management literature and its implications for standard setting. *Accounting Horizons*, 13: 365–383.

Hillman, A. J. and Keim, G. D. 2001. Shareholder value, stakeholder management, and social issues: What's the bottom line? *Strategic Management Journal*, 22: 125–139.

Holthausen, R., Larcker, D., and Sloan, R. 1995. Annual bonus schemes and the manipulation of earnings. *Journal of Accounting and Economics*, 19: 29–74.

Jensen, M. C. 2001. Value maximization, stakeholder theory, and the corporate objective function. In M. Beer and N. Nohria, eds., *Journal of Applied Corporate Finance*, 14(3): 8–21.

Johnson, R. A. and Greening, D. W. 1999. The effects of corporate governance and institutional owenership types on corporate social performance. *Academy of Management Journal*, 42(5): 564–576.

Jensen, M. C. and Meckling, W. 1976. Theory of the firm: managerial behavior, agency costs, and ownership structure. *Journal of Financial Economics*, 3: 305–360.

Kaplan, S. E. 2001. Ethically related judgments by observers of earnings management. *Journal of Business Ethics*, 32: 285–298.

Kaufman, A., Zacharias, L., and Karson, M. 1995. *Managers vs. Owners: The Struggle for Corporate Control in American Democracy*. New York: Oxford University Press.

Kedia, S. 2003. Do executive stock options generate incentives for earnings management?: evidence from accounting restatements. Working paper, Harvard Business School. Boston, MA.

Kim, B. 2002. Adaptation of governance mechanisms to deregulation: a longitudinal study of the US banking industry. Paper presented at the Academy of Management Proceedings. Denver, CO.

Lee, B. B. 2002. Earnings management and equity holdings of CEOs. Paper presented at the Decision Science Institute 2002 Annual Meeting. San Diego, CA.

Levitt, A. Jr. 1998. The number game. *The CPA Journal*, 68: 14–19.

Margolis, J. D. and Walsh, J. P. 2003. Misery loves companies: rethinking social initiatives by business. *Administrative Science Quarterly*, 48(2): 268–305.

McGuire, J. B., Schneeweiss, T., and Sundgren, A. 1988. Corporate social responsibility and firm financial performance. *Academy of Management Journal*, 31(4): 854–872.

McGuire, J. B., Schneeweiss, T., and Sundgren, A. 1990. Perceptions of firm quality: a cause or result of firm performance. *Journal of Management*, 16(1): 167–180.

Merchant, K. A. and Rockness, J. 1994. The ethics of managing earnings: an empirical investigation. *Journal of Accounting and Public Policy*, 13: 79–94.

Mintzberg, H. 1981. Organization design: fashion or fit? *Harvard Business Review*, 59(1): 103–116.

Orlitzky, M., Schmidt, F. I., and Rynes, S. L. 2003. Corporate social and financial performance: a meta-analysis. *Organization Studies*, 24: 403–441.

Pava, M. L. and Krausz, J. 1996. The association between corporate social-responsibility and financial performance: the paradox of social cost. *Journal of Business Ethics*, 15: 321–357.

Richardson, S., Tuma, I., and Wu, M. 2003. Predicting earnings management: the case of earnings restatements. Working paper, University of Michigan. Ann Arbor, MI.

Roman, R. M., Hayibor, S., and Agle, B. R. 1999. The relationship between social and financial performance. *Business & Society*, **38**(1): 109–125.

Sanders, Wm. G. 2001. Behavioral responses of CEOs to stock ownership and stock option pay. *Academy of Management Journal*, **44**(3): 477–492.

Schweitzer, M. E., Ordonez, L., and Douma, B. 2002. The dark side of goal setting: the role of goals in motivating unethical decision making. Paper to be presented at the Academy of Management Annual Meeting. Denver, CO.

St-Onge, S., Magnan, M., Thorne, L., and Raymond, S. 2001. The effectiveness of stock option plans: a field investigation of senior executives. *Journal of Management Inquiry*, **10**(3): 250–266.

Swanson, D. L. 1995. Addressing a theoretical problem by reorienting the corporate social performance model. *Academy of Management Review*, **20**(1): 43–64.

Swanson, D. L. 1999. Toward an integrative theory of business and society: a research strategy for corporate social performance. *Academy of Management Review*, **24**(3): 506–521.

Tristine, J. R. 2003. Sorting through the options: the debate regarding stock options in the wake of recent corporate scandals. *Journal of Deferred Compensation*, **8**(3): 19–30.

Ullman, A. A. 1985. Data in search of a theory: a critical examination of the relationships among social performance, social disclosure and economic performance of US firms. *Academy of Management Journal*, **10**(3): 540–557.

Vogel, T. 2001. Cendant Corp: a case study examining the compensation and accounting issues involved in a stock option repricing program. *Issues in Accounting Education*, **16**(3): 409–435.

Waddock, S. 2000. The multiple bottom lines of corporate citizenship: social investing, reputation, and responsibility audits. *Business and Society Review*, **105**(3): 323–345.

Waddock, S. A. and Graves, S. B. 1997a. The corporate social performance – financial performance link. *Strategic Management Journal*, **18**(4): 303–319.

Waddock, S. A. and Graves, S. B. 1997b. Quality of management and quality of stakeholder relations: are they synonymous? *Business & Society*, **36**(3): 250–279.

Weaver, G. R., Trevino, L. K., and Cochran, P. L. 1999a. Corporate ethics practices in the mid-1990s: an empirical study of the fortune 1000. *Journal of Business Ethics*, **18**: 283–294.

Weaver, G. R., Trevino, L. K., and Cochran, P. L. 1999b. Corporate ethics programs as control systems: influences of executive commitment and environmental factors. *Academy of Management Journal*, **42**(1): 41–57.

Welch, J. 2002. Stock-option cultures: employee ownership in a high-growth software company. Paper presented at the Academy of Management Proceedings. Denver, CO.

Westphal, J. D. and Zajac, E. J. 1994. Substance and symbolism in CEO's long-term incentive plans. *Administrative Science Quarterly*, **39**(3): 367–390.

REPORTS FOR ACCOUNTING RESTATEMENTS

Business Week. 1998. Corporate earnings: who can you trust? September 24, available at: http://www.businessweek.com/1998/40/b3598001.htm.

GAO (US General Accounting Office). 2002. Financial statement restatements: trends, market impacts, regulatory responses, and remaining challenges.

Huron Consulting Group. 2003. An analysis of restatement matters: rules, errors, ethics, for the five years ended December 31, 2002.

Interactive Week. 2001. Tech companies play number game. June 18, 2001.

Ketz, J. E. 2003a. Ebay's unannounced restatement of earnings. SmartPros. Available at: http://www.smartpro.com/x38271.xml.

Ketz, J. E. 2003b. Ebay's stock options: how to transfer wealth from investors to employees. SmartPros. Available at: http://www.smartpro.com/x38271.xml.

3

A Preliminary Investigation into the Association between Canadian Corporate Social Responsibility and Executive Compensation

Lois S. Mahoney
Eastern Michigan University, 406 Owen, 301 W. Michigan Avenue, Ypsilanti, MI 48197

Linda Thorne
York University, 4700 Keele St., North York, Ontario M3J 1P3

Introduction

This chapter conducts a preliminary investigation into the association between executive compensation and corporate social responsibility (CSR) for 58 publicly traded Canadian firms. After controlling for size, we find a significant negative association between salary and CSR and a significant positive relationship between bonus and CSR. We failed to find a relationship between long-term compensation and CSR. Implications for practice and research are discussed.

Keywords: corporate governance, executive compensation, social performance, social responsibility

Corporate social responsibility captures the extent to which firms address social expectations as established by the public (Clarkson, 1995; Griffin & Mahon, 1997; Hillman & Keim, 2001). As Carroll (1979) summarizes, CSR includes a firm's responsibilities to investors and consumers, ethical responsibilities to society, legal responsibility to the government or the law, and discretionary responsibility to the community.

Executive compensation encourages executives to act in ways deemed by a firm's board of directors (Jones, 1995). Compensation can focus executives' efforts. By comparing the association between executive compensation and corporate social responsibility, we consider whether executives' compensation is associated with their concern for social factors and the environment (e.g., Johnson & Greening, 1999; Kane, 2002; McGuire et al., 2003). However, only one previous study has explicitly considered the association between CEO compensation and CSR (i.e., McGuire et al., 2003). McGuire et al. found significant relationships between CSR weakness and salary and CSR weakness and long term compensation. Nevertheless, their reliance on a database that describes the association between compensation and CSR for a single national jurisdiction suggests that additional work is needed.

In this chapter, we explicitly consider whether there is an association between executive compensation and CSR for publicly traded Canadian firms. We use Canada as a basis of our study for two reasons. First, by using Canada, we provide insight into the extent to which previous findings may extend beyond American borders. Second, because Canada and the United States have very similar cultures, intercountry differences arising from differences in culture will be minimized, and differences in findings may be more easily attributed to institutational factors, which differ between the two jurisdictions.

Similar to McGuire et al. (2003), we focus on CEO compensation since the CEO is the only executive who is clearly accountable to the board of directors (and ultimately, to the firm's owners) for overall firm performance. Our sample comprises CEO compensation for 58 Canadian firms trading on the Toronto Stock Exchange (TSE) during 1996. We use a Canadian database that reports CSR at a comprehensive level. Our analysis considers the association between various components of executive compensation, including salary, bonus, and long-term compensation, and it also controls for firm size. Thus, by providing insight into the association between CSR and CEO compensation in Canada, we tap a sophisticated database that provides further insight into the importance of compensation for influencing CSR. We also take a first step in understanding whether executives' compensation may be used to encourage CSR in firms.

This chapter is organized as follows. The next section provides an overview of the literature and the hypotheses presented in this chapter. This is followed by a section on the methods employed and a section on the results obtained and implications. The final section summarizes the key findings.

Hypothesis Development

Salary

Salary is a fixed part of compensation, which generally is considered to have little incentive value as it is not contingent on performance. Nevertheless, the literature suggests a strong association between firm size and salary (Murphy, 1985; Lewellen et al., 1987; Mehran, 1995). We anticipated that larger firms are more politically sensitive to issues such as CSR, and have the resources to address CSR (Watts & Zimmerman, 1986). This in turn suggests that we anticipate a positive association between salary and CSR, due to the positive influence of firm size on compensation.

Hypothesis 1: There is a positive association between salary and CSR.

Due to the importance of size, we also wish to investigate the extent to which salary and CSR are associated after controlling for the size of the firm. However, in keeping with the descriptive nature of this chapter, we do not specifically hypothesize an association.

Bonus and CSR

Bonus is generally considered to be associated with short-term, immediate financial performance (Murphy, 1999). To this end, we anticipate that the greater the bonus, the more the executive would focus on the short term to the detriment of the longer term, which is consistent with the CSR (Kane, 2002). In this vein, McGuire et al. (2003) failed to find an association between bonus and CSR; therefore, we propose the following null hypothesis:

Hypothesis 2: There is no positive association between bonus and CSR.

Long-term Compensation and CSR

Long-term compensation (LTC) provides an executive with the incentive to make decisions that will result in an increase in future stock price. This future potential for wealth accumulation provides the executive with a strong incentive to take action and to make decisions that are consistent with long-term interests (Mehran, 1995), which is consistent with CSR. Accordingly, we anticipate a positive association between long-term contingent executive compensation and CSR (Kane, 2002).

Hypothesis 3: There is a positive association between LTC and total CSR.

Sample Selection

The sample selected for our study comprises the 100 largest Canadian firms, based on TSE market capitalization (i.e., the TSE 100 Index) in 1996. Financial data was obtained from annual financial statements, the Financial Post Information Service Database, and the Globe and Mail. Data on long-term compensation, salary, and other incentives were obtained from the annual proxy statements and from the Blue Book of Canadian Business. Data on corporate social performance were drawn from the Canadian Social Investment Database, CSID, as described below. Missing data reduced the sample size to 58 Canadian firms.

Measures

Measurement of CSR

In this chapter, we measure CSR by the ratings in the CSID, a database of CSR for Canadian firms developed in 1992 by Michael Jantzi Research Associates, Inc. (MJRA).[1] CSR is a comprehensive measure based on the CSID composite measure that reflects key stakeholder relationships that are important emerging influences on corporate strategy (Prahalad & Hamel, 1994) – *community, diversity, employee relations, environment, international, product and business practices,* and *others* (MJRA, 2000).[2] In designing the criteria to rate CSR of firms, MJRA's investment analysts review corporate documents, including each company's annual report, annual information form, and proxy information circular (MJRA, 2003). They also analyze the firm's environmental policy, health and safety policy, and code of business conduct in order to better evaluate the company's performance – see Appendix for further details (Mahoney & Roberts, 2004).

Measurement of Executive Compensation

CEO compensation was used to avoid the potential confounding effect on our results from changes in the mix of executives that may be included through the sample time period. Firms with incomplete data, CEO changes in a given year, nonresident CEOs, and firms with major changes in ownership were dropped from the sample.

---

[1] In their investigation of the association between executive compensation and CSR in the United States, McGuire et al. (2003) relied upon the use of the American database compiled by Kinder, Lydenberg, and Domini (KLD). These two databases are methodologically comparable.

[2] For each of these dimensions, MJRA investigates a range of sources to determine a company score.

Salary

Salary is measured as the annual cash salary paid to an executive during the calendar year in total Canadian dollars.

Bonus and Long-term Compensation

We measure contingent compensation in two ways: bonus and long-term incentives. Bonus rewards an executive through cash compensation in the form of additional incentive payments on an *ex post* basis after performance has been realized. Bonus was calculated as a percentage of the bonus payments to the total compensation for the CEO. Long-term compensation is stock options and restrictive stock awards. Long-term incentives and long-term compensation were calculated as a percentage of stock options and stock option grants, respectively, to the total compensation for the CEO. Stock option grants are valued in dollars using the model proposed by Smith and Zimmerman (1976). The Smith and Zimmerman valuation model attaches a nonnegative value to the options based on their discounted present value at year-end after adjusting for dividends, as discussed in Hemmer (1993),[3] and is particularly appropriate for the valuation of Canadian options as the available information (used in the Black–Scholes model) on debt is not readily available in Canada.

Size

Consistent with prior empirical research on executive compensation, we control for size through the use of sales and return on equity (ROE) (McGuire et al., 1988; McKendall et al., 1999; McWilliams & Siegel, 2000). Similar to McGuire et al. (2003), we used the firm's primary SIC code to control for performances that may vary by industries. The model we use in our analysis to control for size is as follows:

$$\text{CSR}_i = \beta_0 + \beta_1 \text{Salary}_i + \beta_2 \%\text{Bonus}_i + \beta_3 \%\text{LTC}_i \\ + \beta_4 \text{Sales}_i + \beta_5 \text{ROE}_i + \beta_6 \text{Industry}_i \tag{3.1}$$

$$i = \text{firm}$$
$$\beta = \text{regression coefficient}$$

---

[3] The Smith and Zimmerman (1976) model is computed in the following manner: maximum (0, stock price at grant date − present value (exercise price + future value (divident stream compounded at the risk-free rate until option expiration))).

CSR   = corporate social responsibility
Salary   = annual cash salary
%Bonus = bonus payments/total compensation
%LTC   = stock option grants/total compensation
ROE   = net income/owners equity
Sales   = total revenue
Industry = dummy variable

Results

Tables 3.1 presents our primary results, which include the descriptive statistics and the outcome of the correlation analysis. We also include a second analysis, Table 3.2, that controls for size.

As shown in Table 3.1, the mean CSR was 1.66. The average salary was $624,121 and the percentage of bonus to total compensation was 25.2. The percentage of long-term compensation to total compensation was 19.6, and the percentage of bonus and firm size is significantly related to CSR.

In Hypothesis 1 we anticipated a significant positive relationship between salary and CSR, but Table 3.1 fails to find it. However, after controlling for size as in Table 3.2, there is a significant relationship between salary and CSR but in the opposite direction of what we anticipated. Salary is significantly negatively related to CSR. This suggests that the positive association between salary and CSR found in previous research may be attributable to the political pressure exerted on larger firms. But after taking the size factor into account, in fact, the

Table 3.1 Correlations of Pearson correlation matrix with current CSR, compensation, and size

Variable	Mean	SD	1	2	3	4	5
Total CSR	1.66	2.552					
Salary	624,121	243,356	0.105				
% Bonus	0.252	0.185	0.366*	0.182			
% Long-term compensation	0.196	0.212	−0.042	−0.103	−0.366*		
Sales	4,437,697	5,225,266	0.542*	0.546*	0.121	−0.115	
ROE	9.438	10.105	0.325**	0.254	0.457*	−0.106	0.262**

Notes: $*p < .01$; $**p < .05$.

Table 3.2   CSR and compensation in 1996

Explanatory variables	Regression coefficient	Dependent variable: Total CSR
Salary	β_1	$-0.308^a(-2.334)^{b}$**
% Bonus	β_2	0.299(2.199)**
% LTC	β_3	0.123(1.083)
Sales	β_4	0.549(4.110)***
ROE	β_5	0.039(0.300)
Adjusted R^2		0.356
F		3.680**
N		58

Notes: Firm-specific intercepts not reported. *$p < .10$; **$p < .05$; ***$p < .01$, one-tailed.
[a] Standardized regression coefficient; [b] t-statistic

salaries of CEOs at larger firms are not more sensitive to CSR than smaller firms. Further work is needed to assess how the salaries of CEOs at larger and smaller firms differentially respond to CSR.

In Hypothesis 2 we anticipated that we would fail to find a significant positive association between percentage of bonus and CSR. Although the results of our correlation in Table 3.1 is consistent with this hypothesis, after controlling for size, and contrary to our hypothesis, Table 3.2 shows that bonus is significantly related to CSR and that the relationship is a positive one. This suggests again the importance of size for the association between CSR and CEO bonus, and that, in fact, CEO bonus may be more important in influencing CSR.

In Hypothesis 3 we expected to find a significant positive association between LTC and CSR. However, we fail to find support for this association in Tables 3.1 or 3.2.

Implications

Our results may be useful for providing important insights into CSR and corporate governance by suggesting the importance of size in the Canadian arena, and for understanding the importance of factors that influence CSR. Our findings suggest the importance of firm size for the association between CEO compensation and CSR. Firm size is significantly related to CSR in Canada. Before controlling for size, we found a positive association between salary and CSR, and no association between bonus and CSR. However, after controlling for size, higher CEO compensation in the form of salary is negatively associated with CSR and bonus is positively associated with CSR. The results of our analysis are important because they suggest the importance of size and bonus in focusing executives' efforts on CSR.

Nevertheless, our findings are subject to limitations. It is important to recognize that although an independent firm performs the CSID ratings, they are the result of MJRA's definitions and evaluations of CSR. The use of the independent CSID ratings as a measure of CSR has some advantages, but is also limited due to its equal weighting of each of the dimensions of CSR. Further research using different weights for each of the dimensions may prove to be beneficial. In addition, further studies can aid in the development of this research stream by investigating the validity of CSID ratings and providing critiques of MJRA's perspective on CSR.

Our findings also suggest that the association between executive compensation and CSR may not necessarily be similar across national institutional contexts. Additional investigation of the influence of specific institutional factors combined with executive compensation on corporate social actions may be fruitful for understanding how to develop an environment that will encourage higher levels of CSR.

Appendix: Social and environmental rating criteria for MJRA company profiles

Dimension	Strength	Concern
Community issues	Generous giving	Lack of
	Innovative giving	consultation/engagement
	Community consultation/engagement	Breach of covenant
	Strong aboriginal relationships	Weak aboriginal relations
Diversity in workplace	Strong employment equity program	Lack of employment equity initiatives
	Women on board of directors	
	Women in senior management	Employment equity controversies
	Work/family benefits	
	Minority/women contracting	
Employee relations	Positive union relations	Poor union relations
	Exceptional benefits	Safety problems
	Workforce management policies	Workforce reduction
	Cash profit sharing	Inadequate benefits
	Employee ownership/involvement	

Appendix: (Continued)

Dimension	Strength	Concern
Environmental performance	Environmental management strength	Environmental management concern
	Exceptional environment planning and impact assessment	Inadequate environmental planning or impact assessment
	Environmentally sound resource use	Unsound resource use
		Poor compliance record
	Environmental impact reduction	
	Beneficial products and services	Substantial emissions/discharges
		Negative impact of operations
		Negative impact of products
International	Community relations	Poor community relations
	Employee relations	Poor employee relations
	Environment	Poor environmental management/performance
	Sourcing practice	
		Human rights
		Sourcing practices
Product and business practices	Beneficial products and services	Product safety
	Ethical business practices	Pornography
		Marketing practices
		Illegal business practices
Others	Limited compensation	Excessive compensation
	Confidential proxy voting	Dual-class share structure
	Ownership in companies having high CSID Ratings	Ownership in other companies

REFERENCES

Carroll, A. 1979. A three-dimensional conceptual model of corporate social performance. *Academy of Management Review*, 4: 497–505.

Clarkson, M. B. E. 1995. A stakeholder framework for analyzing and evaluating social performance. *Academy of Management Review*, 20(1): 92–117.

Griffin, J. J. and Mahon, J. F. 1997. The corporate social performance and corporate financial performance debate: twenty-five years of incomparable results. *Business and Society*, 36: 5–31.

Hemmer, T. 1993. Risk-free incentive contracts: eliminating agency cost using option-based compensation. *Journal of Accounting and Economics*, **16**: 447–474.

Hillman, A. J. and Keim, G. D. 2001. Shareholder value, stakeholder management, and social issues: what's the bottom line? *Strategic Management Journal*, **22**: 125–139.

Johnson, R. and Greening, D. 1999. The effects of corporate governance and institutional ownership types on corporate social performance. *Academy of Management Journal*, **42**(5): 564–578.

Jones, T. M. 1995. Instrumental stakeholder theory: a synthesis of ethics and economics. *Academy of Management Review*, **20**(2): 404–437.

Kane, E. J. 2002. Using deferred compensation to strengthen the ethics of financial regulation. *Journal of Banking & Finance*, **26**: 1919–1933.

Lewellen, W., Loderer, C., and Martin, K. 1987. Executive compensation and executive incentive problems: an empirical analysis. *Journal of Accounting and Economics*, **9**: 287–310.

Mahoney, L. S. and Roberts, R. 2004. Corporate social performance: empirical evidence on Canadian firms. *Research on Professional Responsibility and Ethics in Accounting*, **9**: 73–99.

McGuire, J., Schneeweis, T., and Sundgren, A. 1988. Corporate social responsibility and firm financial performance. *Academy of Management Journal*, **31**(4): 854–872.

McGuire, J., Dow, S., and Argheyd, K. 2003. CEO incentives and corporate social performance. *Journal of Business Ethics*, **45**(4): 341–359.

McKendall, M., Sanchez, C., and Sicilian, P. 1999. Corporate governance and corporate illegality: the effects of board structure on environmental violations. *International Journal of Organizational Analysis*, **7**(3): 201–223.

McWilliams, A. and Siegel, D. 2000. Corporate social responsibility and financial performance: correlation or misspecification? *Strategic Management Journal*, **21**(5): 603–610.

Mehran, H. 1995. Executive compensation structure, ownership and firm performance. *Journal of Financial Economics*, **38**: 163–184.

MJRA. 2003. http://www.mjra-jsi.com/about.asp?section=1&level_2=0&level_3=0

MJRA. 2000. *Social and Environmental Rating Criteria for MJRA Company Profiles*. Toronto, Ontario: MJRA.

Murphy, K. 1985. Corporate performance and managerial remuneration: an empirical analysis. *Journal of Accounting and Economics*, **7**: 11–42.

Murphy, K. 1999. Executive compensation. In O. Ashenfelter and D. Card, eds., *Handbook of Labor Economics*, Vol. 3, Amsterdam: North-Holland.

Prahalad, C. K. and Hamel, G. 1994. Strategy as a field of study: why search for a new paradigm? *Strategic Management Journal*, **15** (Special Issue): 5–16.

Smith, C. and Zimmerman, J. 1976. Valuing employee stock option plans using option pricing models. *Journal of Accounting Research*, **14**: 357–364.

Watts, R. and Zimmerman, J. 1986. *Positive Accounting Theory*. Englewood Cliffs, NJ: Prentice-Hall.

PART II
Justice-based Analyses of Executive Compensation

Jared Harris provides a broad justice-oriented perspective on the question of executive compensation in "How Much is Too Much?: A Theoretical Analysis of Executive Compensation from the Standpoint of Distributive Justice." Harris considers the question of executive compensation from the point of view of three theories of distributive justice: Rawls's justice-as-fairness perspective, Sen's capabilities approach, and Nozick's libertarian theory of justice. While these three theories of justice differ vastly in important respects, particularly with respect to the distributional outcomes they favor, Harris finds that the three approaches agree in requiring that the *process* of negotiating and setting executive compensation must be fair. Thus, while they may disagree on substantive issues of distributional justice, they find a significant measure of agreement in a requirement of procedural justice.

Like Harris, William H. Shaw considers the question of executive compensation from the perspective of three theories of justice in "Justice, Incentives, and Executive Compensation." Shaw focuses on the question of incentives in executive compensation from perspectives of utilitarianism, libertarianism, and Rawlsian egalitarianism. For Shaw the incentives argument maintains that high levels of executive compensation might be justified on the grounds that those with special talents receive high compensation to induce them to deploy those talents to benefit society. While Shaw finds that the incentives argument appears to be broadly compatible with each of the theories of justice that he considers, radical departures from equal compensation are, nonetheless, quite problematic from the perspective of each theory of justice.

Michael Potts argues that there is much more to consider than merely outcomes or procedures in addressing the question of justice in CEO compensation. For Potts, in "CEO Compensation and Virtue Ethics," issues of virtue matter in a way that precludes considering executive compensation from merely consequentialist or deontological perspectives. Instead, Potts argues that the management of a corporation is a practice in the sense elaborated by Alasdair MacIntyre and applied to business by Robert Solomon. If that is correct, the virtuous CEO would recognize the requirements of a leadership role in the community that is the firm, along with a requirement of self-restraint in seeking personal compensation.

In her chapter, "Chihuahuas in the Gardens of Corporate Capitalism: A Discussion," Lyla D. Hamilton locates the core issue of executive compensation in the relationship between the firm's board of directors and the firm's top management. As such, she locates the central problem of executive compensation within the locus of promise-keeping. Specifically, Hamilton argues that the "Chihuahuas" that are corporate directors fail to restrain the firm's top management and that they thus fail to keep the promises that they made to the firm's shareholders. While not ignoring issues of distributive justice as they apply to executive compensation, Hamilton believes that the issue of failed promises is logically prior and points the way to a potential resolution of the executive compensation debate.

4

How Much is Too Much? A Theoretical Analysis of Executive Compensation from the Standpoint of Distributive Justice

Jared Harris
Department of Strategic Management & Organization, Carlson School of Management, University of Minnesota

In analyzing the ethics of executive compensation, this paper examines the issue from the standpoint of three prominent theories of distributive justice. Applying each of these "ideal" theories to the question of how to structure CEO pay illustrates a variety of different objections and considerations. Surveying the theories together in one analysis – rather than considering each one independently – reveals a certain amount of common ground among them. The theoretical analysis reveals a convergent conclusion about the importance of open and fair executive selection and compensation-setting *processes* to the establishment of an ethically appropriate level of executive pay.

Keywords: executive compensation, distributive justice, business ethics, political philosophy, stakeholder theory

Introduction

The level of executive pay has skyrocketed over the past several decades, widening the gap between the compensation of CEOs[1] and that of typical organizational employees. Although there exists a traditional underlying rationale for highly

---

[1] In this chapter, I use the terms "executive" and "CEO" interchangeably.

paid executives within the corporate community, the business validity of high CEO pay is coming under increasing scrutiny. In addition, there is a rising tide of opposition to lavish executive compensation from outside the business community that also suggests such compensation as objectionable. But on what grounds are such objections based? How much is too much? Although exorbitant amounts of executive remuneration might simply seem absurd from a common sense standpoint – especially to corporate outsiders – an analysis that incorporates the major theories of distributive justice is extremely useful in framing a more comprehensive, normative picture of executive pay. Rather than an in-depth treatise on one particular political philosophy, this chapter surveys three major theories of distributive justice, applying them each specifically to the question of how corporate executives ought to be paid.

Background

Executive pay has recently increased dramatically, widening the disparity between the compensation of top managers and typical workers (Lublin, 1996; Young, 1998; Useem, 2003). The notion that managers should be given sizeable incentives in order to increase a company's chance for success has a long history (e.g., Patton, 1951), and its continued prevalence reflects a "best practice" promoted by business academics and consultants. For example, Jensen and Murphy (1990) issued a well-known call for increased CEO incentive compensation via stock options, warning that otherwise, executives would behave as bureaucrats. As if in answer to this call, total compensation for executives in the United States steadily rose over the next decade, jumping from 100 times the pay of a typical worker in 1990 to somewhere between 350 and 570 times the pay of a typical worker, primarily through the use of stock options (Rynes & Gerhart, 2000; Hall & Murphy, 2003). Whether or not this trend is attributable to the influence of specific commentators, the underlying rationale for increased executive pay has remained the same, namely, increased contingent pay – when tied to a firm's stock price – is the best way to "align the incentives" of stockholders and top managers.

Aligning the incentives of these two groups is a sought-after attempt to solve the "agency problem" of executives pursuing their own interests at shareholders' expense (Jensen & Meckling, 1976). Managers, in other words, ought to be given incentives to increase economic returns to shareholders. Some scholars (e.g., Friedman, 1970) argue – from what is essentially a property rights perspective – that this represents an absolute fiduciary duty; managers must *only* and *always* act in the interest of those shareholder owners. In this tradition, others (e.g., Jensen, 2002) buttress this argument by explicitly suggesting the presence of the underlying utilitarian notion that maximizing shareholder profits is the way to improve a society's overall social welfare; from this point of view, high levels of executive pay are merely a way to ultimately achieve the greatest good for the greatest number, and the ends justify the means.

However, a number of economic experts and business academics are questioning the effectiveness of incentive pay in resolving the agency problem and providing the desirable business and societal outcomes. For instance, Bebchuk and Fried (2003) argue that, while executive compensation is typically viewed as a potential solution to the agency problem, it is in fact likely to be part of the agency problem. In this sense, excessive pay for executives may actually cause, rather than solve, managerial problems. Noted economist Hal Varian (2002) recently recognized that, given the powerful incentive provided by stock options, "the temptation to inflate stock prices artificially will also be strong." Nobel Laureate Joseph Stiglitz argues that high-powered incentives and stock options give executives "more incentive to misreport (corporate) incomes" (Meyers, 2003). In support of these ideas, researchers have empirically examined the link between high levels of CEO incentive compensation and the likelihood of financial misrepresentation, finding that such malfeasance is increasingly likely as the level of incentive compensation rises (Harris & Bromiley, 2003; O'Connor et al., 2003).

In addition to this emerging view from the scholarly community, it appears that the tide of public opinion also largely opposes ballooning executive pay. In the aftermath of several years of large corporate scandals – many involving executive compensation – a diverse range of voices are increasingly expressing their objection to large CEO rewards. In a recent study, for example, focus groups comprised of "ordinary Americans" expressed outrage over burgeoning CEO pay, especially during times of employee cutbacks – citing greed as the source of the problem (Farkas et al., 2004). For a more specific case, consider the ousting of former New York Stock Exchange executive Richard Grasso, who was not only forced to resign over the size of his compensation package, but is now being sued by the state of New York for the recovery of a portion of that "unreasonable" pay (Thomas, 2004).

Yet despite the abundant attention and dialogue given to this issue, the questions remain: What determines whether or not a certain level of executive compensation is reasonable? How can a justifiable level of CEO pay be determined? In order to advance the discussion and provide some tentative answers, I analyze the issue of executive compensation from the standpoint of distributive justice, drawing upon three core theories of several notable political philosophers. Although each theory raises slightly different objections to exorbitant executive pay, they interestingly lead to a convergent conclusion about how CEO compensation ought to be determined.

Analysis

An analysis of the implications of distributive justice for executive compensation would be incomplete without examining the field's most important theories, including John Rawls' theory of justice as fairness (1971), the capabilities-based approach of Amartya Sen (1999) and Martha Nussbaum (2000), and the libertarian theory of Robert Nozick (1974). Although all of these works are ideal theories, they are invaluable in framing a variety of substantive objections to lavish executive pay. Understanding these theoretical objections in turn paves the way to a normative conception about how executive pay ought to be structured. Since none of the theories claims to be a "complete" or "full" theory, each of them is considered in turn, in an effort to construct an integrative conception of the challenges and potential solutions associated with the structuring of executive compensation. This integrative discussion follows the three respective theoretical analyses.

This theoretical study of the ethics of executive compensation, as outlined, could be conducted at several different levels of analysis. For example, using the ideal theories as a framework might immediately call to mind a host of expansive, global considerations for multicultural political economy and the role of the state in multinational business and societal infrastructure. However, the approach taken here is a stricter, more focused level of analysis centering on the firm and its primary stakeholders (Freeman, 1984). Since the firm's principal stakeholders include shareholders, employees, customers, suppliers, and the social community in which the organization resides (Phillips, 2003), an analysis of the distributive justice implications of executive compensation within this "mini-society" provides a meaningful boundary condition on the analysis without limiting the dialectical nature of the contrasting stakeholder interests. A stakeholder analysis of executive compensation, therefore, serves as a useful model for a greater societal analysis, but also helps to bridge the gap between abstract ethical ideals and practical business constraints (Sen, 1997). In the context of this chapter, the analysis also serves to apply and extend stakeholder theory.

Justice as Fairness

Through the use of a carefully conceived thought experiment called the "original position," John Rawls derives two fundamental principals of justice. These are the key criteria in establishing distributive justice. Therefore, the critical task of a

Rawlsian analysis of executive compensation is to determine which, if either, of these principles is likely to be violated in situations of high CEO pay, and if so, under what circumstances. Although Rawls articulates the two principles in a variety of slightly different ways, his initial formulation of them reads as follows:

> First: each person is to have an equal right to the most extensive scheme of equal basic liberties compatible with a similar scheme of liberties for others.
>
> Second: social and economic inequalities are to be arranged so that they are both (a) reasonably expected to be to everyone's advantage, and (b) attached to positions and offices open to all. (1971: 53)

I focus on the second of Rawls' principles, since the most intuitive objections arise from this principle, with its two parts. In fact, the first part (or "difference principle") is what many common objectors to high CEO pay appeal to – perhaps unknowingly – in voicing objections based on, for example, the disparity between executive and entry worker salaries. The objection, in Rawls' framework, is that at least some of the least well off among the corporation's stakeholders – in this case, hourly workers – are not really made any better off by handsomely paying the CEO. Such an objection can certainly be applied to other stakeholder groups; for example, high executive pay is also seen as a drain on returns that could otherwise be returned to shareholders (e.g., Bavaria, 1991; Monks & Minow, 2004: 262–274). The "least well off" among a firm's stakeholders may also include customers, suppliers, and the social community in which the organization resides, for which the same question remains salient: from the standpoint of the difference principle, is a high amount of CEO pay defensible if the least well off would benefit from the CEO being paid less?

An analysis of the difference principle, then, quickly becomes a question of allocation – whether a certain dollar amount is best paid to the CEO, or distributed in some other fashion to the firm's stakeholders. If it could be shown that an arrangement to pay the firm's executive $100 million in annual compensation leads to at least slightly better pay for the lowest paid worker – or to marginally better quality in the consumer product produced, or to slight increases in the public goods of the community in which the firm resides – than other pay arrangements in which the CEO receives less, then the difference principle might be satisfied. Those who defend high levels of executive pay often argue that this is in fact the case, invoking the social welfare argument that a rising tide lifts all boats. In other words, incentives at the top should create benefits at the bottom, and in the process of doing so, satisfy the demands of both Friedman and Rawls. The presumed mechanism for such a process is that executives with proper incentives will raise the overall performance level of the organization, leading to greater profits that not only reward the CEO, but also trickle down to the least well off among the firm's stakeholders.

One gap in such a defense of high executive pay is that there is no real mechanism for the trickle down. Why should we assume that *increased* profits would be any more likely to distribute down to non-executive stakeholders than profits that are *not* increased? Setting that aside, the even greater problem is that a number of studies have had difficulty showing a link between executive incentive pay and better performance for the firm (Murphy, 1999; Mishra et al., 2000; Blasi & Kruse, 2003)[2], and some even show that it leads to fraud or financial misrepresentation (Harris & Bromiley, 2003; O'Connor et al., 2003; Schnatterly, 2003). So regardless of whether or not there is any mechanism to more justly distribute increased profits to various stakeholders, it is not at all clear that handsome rewards for executives lead to a general increase in profits in the first place. The tide may not be rising at all. Unless such a clear connection can be shown, along with some level of visibility into the corresponding mechanism intended to distribute some portion of the gains to the firm's stakeholders who are least well off, instances of high levels of executive pay are likely to violate the difference principle.

Rawls' second principle of justice also encompasses, in addition to the difference principle, the notion of "open position," or fair equality of opportunity. I argue that high levels of executive compensation are likely to be associated with a violation of this aspect of Rawls' theory as well. Because Rawls himself stipulates that the standard of open position have priority over the difference principle, this means that – from the standpoint of justice as fairness – an executive compensation arrangement violating fair equality of opportunity is even more problematic than one whose objection arises only from the difference principle.

Whereas applying the difference principle to executive compensation issues would focus on the distribution of wealth to executives versus the stakeholders who are least well off, applying the open position standard to questions of

---

[2] Not only is there no clear link between high executive incentive pay and positive firm performance, some studies indicate worse performance. For example, Blasi and Kruse (2003) find that from 1993 to 2001, the one quarter of companies that gave the smallest shares of options to top management gave their investors a 31.3% annual return. Shareholders of the one quarter of companies that gave disproportionately to top executives received only a 22.5% return. In addition, related work on costly managerial perquisites also supports this idea; Yermack (2004) finds that CEOs' personal use of company aircraft is associated with substantial and significant under-performance of their firms' stocks.

executive compensation is primarily concerned with how such pay is determined, and whether or not the CEO position itself is truly accessible to all. One may, as Rawls explains, construe a motive for open position based upon an efficient application of the difference principle – that fair equality of opportunity is the efficient way to find the most talented person for a particular job, who will then tend to do the best job possible in that position, in turn benefiting everyone else the most, including the least well off – but Rawls clearly rejects this notion in favor of a much more primal reason to uphold the ideal of open position:

> if some places were not open on a basis fair to all, those kept out would be right in feeling unjustly treated even though they benefited from the greater efforts of those who were allowed to hold them. They would be justified in their complaint not only because they were excluded from certain external rewards of office but because they were debarred from experiencing the realization of self which comes from a skillful and devoted exercise of social duties. They would be deprived of one of the main forms of human good. (1971: 73)

Therefore, an analysis of an executive compensation arrangement from the standpoint of justice as fairness must not only look at the compensatory distribution itself, but also address whether or not the determination of the CEO's pay – as well as the very process of selecting that executive in the first place – satisfies the standard of fair equality of opportunity.

With respect to the actual filling of executive positions, anecdotal accounts of conflicts of interest, revolving door hiring practices, and closely interlocking boards of directors – where one CEO serves on another's board, and vice versa – suggest a system that appears to favor reciprocity as much as ability. Such ideas have found scholarly support; for instance, Davis et al. (2003) explore evidence that corporate America is overseen by a relatively small network of executives who to a great extent have social connections or acquaintances in common – and that these board ties have a big impact on issues of corporate governance. One of these issues is the setting of executive pay; compensation committee members with close relationships to CEOs have been shown to be typically more benevolent in awarding compensation than those members with more distant relationships (Young & Buchholtz, 2002), suggesting the presence of strong norms of reciprocity within the boardroom. Westphal and Khanna (2003) study the downside of ignoring such norms, finding that board members who act to defy or limit CEOs' power are subject to sanctions and ostracism. Consequently, while believers in corporate meritocracy might be more sanguine about the chances of those with more ability consistently rising to the top, the picture is at best mixed. At the least, it could scarcely be argued that all (or even most) executive positions are filled in a way that makes the opportunity truly accessible to all.

Furthermore, once appointed, how is an executive's compensation determined? Although some have suggested that handsome compensation duly rewards the complexity of the executive's duties (Henderson & Fredrickson, 1996) or mitigates the CEO's personal risk (Chung & Charoenwong, 1991), consider some of the other factors that have been shown to positively influence the size of executive pay packages: CEO celebrity or notoriety (Rosen, 1981; Porac et al., 1999; Hayward et al., 2004), "bandwagoning" or the use of popular management techniques (Staw & Epstein, 2000), and the dominance of insiders or friends on an executive's compensation committee (Conyon & Peck, 1998). In addition to such insiders, the executives themselves routinely sit on their own compensation committees, essentially facilitating pay packages for themselves of ever-increasing generosity. I suggest Rawls might say that such things are clear indications that the demands of fair equality of opportunity have been frustrated.

One way this might be commonly envisioned is in terms of the value proposition of the CEO to the firm; presumably, one of the outcomes of true fair equality of opportunity is that the best person should ultimately get the job. Granted, Rawls supports open position not because such a person would better "deserve" the corresponding rewards, but rather because such a process is essential to the Rawlsian conception of what is valuable to humans. Yet when viewed from the reverse direction, the value proposition lens might lend insight; someone who is being compensated beyond what their talents reasonably deserve is very likely the product of a selection process that violates open position. So while the existence of an executive who is clearly qualified for (or "worth") a large pay package is not necessarily a guarantee that the process was open, a CEO who is clearly overpaid relative to his or her endowments is a signal that the process has somehow shortchanged fair equality of opportunity. The difficulty, of course, remains in identifying an answer to the initial question of whether a given CEO is in fact overcompensated. Justice as fairness provides one potential framework for beginning to resolve this question.

In a recent cartoon (see Figure 4.1), the character Alice confronts her CEO on this very issue: is there reasonable justification for his excessive pay? Although Alice is immediately satisfied when she sees the CEO produce a golden egg, justice as fairness would require additional inquiry. In order for us to know if the compensation package for the gold-producing executive satisfies the difference principle, we need to verify that the least well off among the firm's stakeholders

Figure 4.1   Golden eggs and appropriate CEO pay (Used by permission).

stands to benefit more from the arrangement than from some other executive pay structure. In order for us to know if the compensation package of the gold-producing executive satisfies fair equality of opportunity, we need to establish whether the process for selecting him and setting his compensation was just and accessible to all. Was the CEO position open to other people with the ability to lay golden eggs? Would any of the other egg layers produce the same amount of eggs for a lesser compensation package? Or was this particular egg-laying CEO simply more of a celebrity, or did he have friends or sympathizers on the board's hiring and compensation committees? These are the types of questions that need to be examined with respect to real-world compensation scenarios, in order to determine what kind of pay is justified for business executives according to justice as fairness. In conducting such an analysis, the two key tests – and consequently Rawls' biggest potential objections – in establishing a morally justified executive pay package are the difference principle and the standard of open position.

The Capabilities Approach

Amartya Sen and Martha Nussbaum approach questions of distributive justice somewhat differently from Rawls. For example, their perspectives are much more intuitionist in nature than the constructivist approach of justice as fairness. Although their conception of the person is roughly similar to that of Rawls, it includes some ideas that are almost Aristotelian; a conception that views people as agents who have a hand in their own destiny, who have many and diverse interests, who require freedom to achieve their own version of a valuable life, and who are all equally interested in and deserving of such ideals. As such, these theorists' approaches to human development and justice center primarily on human capabilities and freedoms.[3] Freedoms, in this view, are essentially the capabilities to do the things that are central to this conception of personal development and fulfillment. In their respective treatises, both Sen and Nussbaum explore their principles largely within the context of the developing third world, but as with the prior discussion of Rawls, I here adopt the more narrow boundary condition of applying their ideas to executive compensation within the context of a company's primary stakeholders.

Analyzing executive compensation from the standpoint of the capabilities approach essentially means that one must view CEO pay through a singular critical lens: in terms of its role in capability enhancement or deprivation for the firm's stakeholders. In general, such an analysis boils down to the following assessment: if the capabilities of a firm's stakeholders do not currently meet an adequate threshold, then it will be very hard to justify additional or excess compensation for the firm's executive.

Therefore, the critical question then becomes: what are the freedoms or capabilities that should be considered? Sen proposes five different types of instrumental freedoms that lead to the development of valuable human capabilities: political freedoms, economic facilities, social opportunities, transparency guarantees, and protective security (1999: 39–40). Nussbaum takes a slightly different angle in identifying the essential capabilities themselves; she categorizes them into 10 different areas: (1) life, (2) bodily health, (3) bodily integrity, (4) senses, imagination, and thought, (5) emotions, (6) practical reason, (7) affiliation, (8) co-existence with other species and the natural world, (9) play and recreation, and (10) control over one's political and material environment (2000: 78–80).

One of the key themes of the capabilities approach, as made clear by the authors' broad lists of the essential capabilities and freedoms, is that income (or economic wealth) alone is an insufficient way to conceive of and measure human well-being. From this standpoint, any distribution of economic wealth should be predicated on – and valued for – the ability of such income to facilitate needed capability enhancements for individuals. Yet individuals clearly vary in their own personal circumstances and physical characteristics; they also exist within varying

---

[3] Despite fine-grained differences in the theories of Sen and Nussbaum, they are sufficiently similar and complementary that I consider them together for purposes of this chapter.

environmental conditions and social climates (Sen, 1999: 70–71). This means that:

> The contrast between the different perspectives of income and capability has a direct bearing on the space in which inequality and efficiency are to be examined. For example, a person with high income but no opportunity of political participation is not "poor" in the usual sense, but is clearly poor in terms of an important freedom. Someone who is richer than most others but suffers from an ailment that is very expensive to treat is obviously deprived in an important way, even though she would not be classified as poor in the usual statistics of income distribution. A person who is denied the opportunity of employment but given a handout from the state as an "unemployment benefit" may look a lot less deprived in the space of incomes than in terms of the valuable – and valued – opportunity of having a fulfilling occupation. (Sen, 1999: 93–94)

While highlighting the intuitive attractiveness of appealing to human capabilities in deciding questions of distributive justice, this also indirectly highlights one of the challenges in applying the capabilities approach: because of the wide heterogeneity of personal situations and conditions, it is difficult to be sure when a threshold level of functioning has actually been realized. It is also unclear – assuming the possibility of a situation in which such a basic threshold capability level is nominally achieved by all relevant stakeholders – what the distributive ordering scheme should then be, and what the duties for distribution and capability enhancement are at that point.[4] Sen and Nussbaum would likely contend that such an optimistic scenario is highly unlikely, even within the boundaries of an American corporation and its stakeholders; and if so, some of the money earmarked for executive pay might otherwise be put to use in offsetting capability deprivations or enhancing the positive freedoms of the firm's other stakeholders.

Therefore, from the vantage point of the capability approach to distributive justice, the primary objection to high CEO pay will arise when a company executive is being highly compensated while other stakeholders are languishing below a baseline level of human functioning. In order to levy such an objection, one

---

[4] By focusing on the developing third world, Sen and Nussbaum forestall the immediate need for them to address such questions of ordering. They illustrate their theoretical points with clear and obvious examples of capability impoverishment and gross limitations on freedoms, essentially asserting that, given the abundance of such massive capability deprivations throughout the world, an additional, nuanced consideration of a distribution to those already possessing an adequate threshold level of functioning is a secondary task. This creates a challenge for an analysis like this one, where such parity may be a more achievable state than Sen and Nussbaum envision in their ideal, global theory.

would have to directly examine the capabilities of the firm's stakeholders. For example, if contract workers in an overseas manufacturing facility are being subjected to unsafe working conditions, or are not being paid a living wage, then several of their primary human freedoms are likely to be in jeopardy. Alternatively, if a domestic employee, a single mother, is given a difficult work schedule and a low level of compensation such that it is difficult for her to financially and emotionally care for her handicapped daughter, then several important capabilities might clearly not be met. If a firm's factory emissions are contaminating a community's water supply or air quality at levels that endanger or degrade human health, residents of that community suffer from a certain amount of capability deprivation.

Within the capabilities framework, these are precisely the types of considerations to contemplate in deciding how large the CEO's annual compensation should be. This view highlights an organization's obligation to attempt to enhance the capability needs of the firm's other stakeholders. For example, the firm's responsibility to address the capability needs of the employee stakeholder group could be envisioned as follows:

> Organizations . . . have an obligation to provide work and compensation that leave employees with the energy, autonomy, will, and income to pursue meaning at work and a meaningful life outside of work. (Ciulla, 2000: 226)

Assuming that one can recognize whether various stakeholders' freedoms are inadequate, as well as how the insufficient capabilities in question might be enhanced, large amounts of CEO pay are problematic; portions of a $300 million compensation package are likely to go a long way toward offsetting a host of capability problems among a firm's other stakeholders, be they shareholders, employees, community residents, suppliers, or customers. Indeed this would be a moral obligation, from a capabilities approach standpoint. This constitutes the primary objection to high executive pay within the capabilities framework: to the extent that other stakeholders are deficient in realizing essential human freedoms, high amounts of CEO compensation should be redistributed in a meaningful, capabilities-enhancing way.

In addition to this central objection, I draw attention to another specific objection that arises from one of the particular areas of human capability. Hiring and compensation in the executive suite will run afoul of the capabilities approach to the extent that the filling of executive position and setting of pay level is an opaque process hinging on social connections, rather than an open process decided on merit and ability. Similar to the Rawlsian standard of fair equality of opportunity, the capabilities framework for distributive justice requires that individuals have "the right to seek employment on an equal basis with others" (Nussbaum, 2000: 80). In other words, if high levels of executive pay are an indicator that the CEO "old boy's club" is exclusive and favors the advancement of cronies while limiting the opportunity for other qualified candidates to seek executive positions, then justice will have been compromised. As with the Rawlsian objection of open position, a closed hiring process affects the actual stakeholders of the organization to the extent that it escalates pay for the executive and – in this case – shifts resources from other initiatives that might otherwise be capability enhancing. Central to this argument is the notion that income is important only to the extent that it enables capability enhancement, and in that sense is essentially a means to an end. There is no argument within the capability approach for income transfer solely for the purpose of wealth accumulation; in fact, there are clear examples of a disconnect between the two, wherein wealth transfer alone is not able to sufficiently mitigate a capability deprivation. Sen's (1999: 28) purpose in discussing the case of well-cared-for slave laborers who chose freedom over income, for example, is to accentuate that human capabilities are much more important than money, and that one does not always lead to the other. Therefore, this particular capabilities-based objection relates to high executive pay only with respect to what it might represent: a closed process of filling the executive positions in the first place. In order to satisfy the demands of the capabilities approach, such positions should be open to all, providing each potential candidate for an executive position – as with all candidates for other, non-executive positions – an "equal starting place" from which to prove their merits for the position (Werhane & Radin, 2004: 171).

In summary, the capabilities approach entails several requirements that constitute two potential objections to the way executives are employed and compensated. These might be summarized into two questions: (1) Is the executive highly paid, despite other stakeholder capability deficiencies? and (2) Is the level of executive pay an indicator that the process of CEO selection is something less than an open process, providing equal opportunity to all? From the standpoint of the capabilities approach, these are the questions that need to be examined with respect to real-world scenarios, in order to determine what kind of hiring practices and pay are justified for business executives.

Libertarian Theory

In his theory of distributive justice, Robert Nozick (1974) focuses primarily on liberty with respect to property, for the most part leaving other capabilities and considerations out of his theory. Nozick argues, essentially, that nothing beyond

a so-called minimalist state – that protects its members from force or fraud – is justified. The base assumptions of Nozick's libertarianism are justice in acquisition
and justice in transfer. In fact, these assumptions really represent the very core
of the theory, and are the replacement for other "patterned history" schemes of
distributive justice that are represented, in Nozick's view, by other nonlibertarian
theories (e.g., 1974: 156–157). Simply put, if everyone is justly entitled to the distribution of property they actually have – that is, the goods have been obtained
through "justice-preserving" means of acquisition and transfer – then the demands
of justice are satisfied and there is no further need to examine distribution
amounts, inequities, or redistributions (1974: 151). Assuming an initial fair distribution, free market forces are proposed as the best way to govern future transfers, and
actual distribution inequities are irrelevant as long as they are fair.

On the other hand, Nozick explicitly raises the point that, in the real world,
these underlying assumptions sometimes do not hold:

> Some people steal from others, or defraud them, or enslave them, seizing their
> product and preventing them from living as they choose, or forcibly exclude others
> from competing in exchanges. None of these are permissible models of transition
> from one situation to another. And some persons acquire holdings by means not
> sanctioned by the principle of justice in acquisition. (1974: 152)

He goes on to explain how these problems give rise to the sticky dilemma of past
injustices and how to correct for such things. Despite raising this issue, however,
Nozick quickly retreats back to the territory of his ideal theory, offering as a
solution only the mere possibility of an unspecified "principle of rectification"
that would "presumably" remedy such situations (1974: 152–153).

Although this raises a number of interesting theoretical questions, further
analysis of Nozick's libertarianism is unnecessary because at this point we already
have a clear picture of his potentially strong objection to CEO compensation:
that the determination and distribution of such compensation might not meet
the standards of justice in acquisition and justice in transfer. All of the subsequent
libertarian tenets – individual responsibility, free and unfettered market transfer
mechanisms, individual consumer liberty – cannot even be meaningfully applied
to questions of executive compensation if the process of paying CEOs violates
justice in acquisition or transfer. These underlying principles must hold in order
for Nozick's theory to have any further analytical efficacy. If these principles can
be shown to have been violated in the case of a particular executive's overly-
generous pay package, then they become the libertarian viewpoint's primary
objection to that particular instance of a high level of executive compensation.

In this view, the process for determining and distributing executive compensation must be just. Because Nozick argues that a thief is not entitled to his ill-gotten gains, it follows that executives who use an insider's advantage to enrich themselves at the expense of other stakeholders also do not attain just entitlement; such a situation scarcely looks like free exercise of liberty in action. From this standpoint, it is not the disparity (or result) of the pay distribution that fuels the objection; rather, the process that is less than fair and transparent. Recall the case of Richard Grasso; the state of New York is attempting to recover a portion of Grasso's compensation because he is perceived to have allegedly exploited his position by deceiving his compensation committee about the details of his pay package (Thomas, 2004), a process deemed to be unfair. Although some might casually invoke Nozick's famous Wilt Chamberlain thought experiment[5] to defend those (like many CEOs) who receive large incomes, a close examination reveals that the key mechanism in this example is the unfettered, fully informed liberty exercised by the fans who willingly, freely choose to pay extra in order to watch Wilt play. It is an ultimate stylized example of a free market in action. In contrast, it is hard to imagine a similar libertarian defense of Wilt's extra income distribution under altered hypothetical conditions, in which the extra income is channeled to Wilt via back-door dealing or unjust appropriation – an arrangement that his fans would undoubtedly object to, were they aware of it. Therefore, to the extent that an executive compensation-setting process falls short of attaining true liberty, transparency, and voluntary acquiescence by the stakeholders concerned, the libertarian framework suggests that such a process is unjust.

There is an additional libertarian objection that arises from Nozick's theory, unrelated to the objection of unjust process, which is also suggested by the example of Wilt Chamberlain. In this example, Wilt's extra earning power at the ticket office arises because he is "greatly in demand by basketball teams," presumably because of his unique – or at least, extraordinary – abilities as a player (Nozick, 1974: 161). A legitimate question is whether such an example can be generalized to situations of corporate executives.[6] Undoubtedly, many executives would

---

[5] The example is used by Nozick to show the futility and irrelevance of an appeal to equality of *distribution*; in the hypothetical example, Wilt Chamberlain signs a contract to the local team by which he gets an extra 25 cents for each ticket sold. One million spectators buy tickets that season, resulting in extra payments to Wilt of $250,000. Nozick argues that nothing is wrong with this inequity; Wilt is fully entitled to that extra distribution because the fans voluntarily transferred it to him, and were happy to pay the sum in return for the pleasure of watching him play.

[6] Ronald Dworkin (2000: 111–112) argues that the Wilt Chamberlain example – while acceptable in its stylized form – is scarcely generalizable at all to any actual, real-world societal contexts.

argue in the affirmative. Yet the cartoon with Alice and the golden egg-laying CEO suggests – albeit in a tongue-in-cheek way – that executives may not in fact be worth their exorbitant pay unless they can do something as incredible as lay golden eggs.

This echoes the "value proposition" point of view discussed earlier in connection with Rawls' principle of fair equality of opportunity. Ignoring for a moment the question of whether the distribution process is just, at the very least we ought to critically question whether extremely well-paid CEOs truly bring unique – or even extraordinary – value to their positions. The answer may be in some cases yes, and in other cases no, but generally speaking, it is far less clear that highly paid corporate executives embody the kind of exceptional value proposition represented by Wilt in the stylized example. In fact, executives are often paid well regardless of poor corporate performance (e.g., Mishra et al., 2000), and even – through the use of "golden parachute" exit contracts – in situations where they leave in disgrace (Brin, 2002; Lublin & Hechinger, 2002). The notion of connecting CEO compensation to an appropriate value proposition is an essential part of the complaint against Grasso: the exchange was led by other competent leaders prior to him, is currently being led by a new competent leader, and although he may have provided solid leadership, he was ultimately too replaceable to command such inordinately high remuneration (Surowiecki, 2003). In other words, Nozick's thought experiment would hardly make any sense at all if he had chosen to illustrate it with a third-string, unknown collegiate player instead of a storied professional superstar like Wilt Chamberlain.[7]

The assumptions of justice in acquisition and justice in transfer provide the foundation for Nozick's libertarian theory of distributive justice, requiring that the processes of executive compensation determination and distribution – if they are to be considered morally defensible – be just and fair. In addition, the primacy of liberty and market mechanisms within the theory demand that executives be not paid beyond their value proposition. From a libertarian perspective, these are the critical factors that need to be examined with respect to actual executive compensation scenarios, in order to determine what kind of pay levels are justified for particular business executives.

---

[7] Alternatively, if one strongly believes in the efficacy of free market mechanisms, as Nozick does, the value proposition objection could also be envisioned simply as another aspect of the just process objection. If the market mechanisms for CEO compensation were truly free, transparent, and unfettered, then executives would only be able to command the incomes commensurate with their true value propositions. If the processes of acquisition and transfer could be trusted to be just, then the problem of CEOs being paid beyond their value proposition might theoretically take care of itself.

Discussion and Conclusions

The three major theories of distributive justice highlighted in this chapter raise a number of potential objections to high levels of executive compensation. This is not surprising, given that the theories arise from widely divergent political philosophies. In common political parlance, for example, the three frameworks – fairness doctrines, human development efforts, and libertarian approaches to policy – are generally seen as being very different in their standard dogma and perceived ramifications. One might expect such substantially different theories of distributive justice to produce starkly contrasting critiques or conclusions with respect to a specific issue like executive compensation. In academic research, strong conclusions are often drawn from one theoretical framework, because multi-theoretic analyses of specific issues can result in an intractable stalemate. Indeed, other multi-perspective philosophical analyses of executive compensation have proven inconclusive (Nichols & Subramaniam, 2001).

It is therefore a constructive outcome of the analysis that such a strong common theme emerges from applying each of these three ideal theories to the question of justice in executive compensation. In this case, each theory produces a central requirement that the *processes* governing executive selection and/or compensation be just; otherwise, high levels of pay for executives cannot be justified. In Rawls' theory of justice as fairness, this arises from the principle of fair equality of opportunity. Similarly, the capabilities approach to human development requires the essential human freedom to seek employment on equal basis with others. From Nozick's libertarian vantage point, justice in acquisition and transfer must undergird all distributions of wealth or property in order for one's entitlement claim to be justified. It is clear from these theoretical objections that the processes of choosing and setting compensation for executives must approximate the type of fair, open, market mechanisms that would satisfy all three frameworks.

A closely related way of envisioning this theme emerges from Rawls and Nozick: that executives should be paid commensurate with the true value proposition they bring to the organization. For justice as fairness, executives paid beyond their true value proposition will be objectionable to the extent that their compensation level arises from the standard of fair equality of opportunity having been compromised. In a similar manner, a libertarian framework allows for extraordinary performers to receive exceptional incomes, provided that those individuals are indeed truly outstanding and the associated income transfer represents a fully informed choice. In this sense, one of the outcomes of a just process for selecting executives and determining their pay is a more open and accurate appraisal of their value propositions.

The questions then become: to what extent is this convergent theoretical objection to unjust processes in CEO selection and compensation a valid one in today's actual world of executive pay? And if so, what can be done? One indication of the validity of this theoretical concern is the corresponding evidence from management scholars, some of which was previously discussed in this analysis. In some cases, these studies shed an unflattering light on a process that is beset with conflicts of interest and reciprocal currying of favors. In other cases, the evidence is less damning but still serves to illuminate a process that appears to be inadequately transparent, open, or free. All of this means that we may be "kidding ourselves" by assuming that "free enterprise is at work in our boardrooms when it really is not" (Bavaria, 1991: 11). Although the prevalence of discernible process problems does not imply their universality, it does suggest that significant numbers of boardrooms fall short of meeting a standard that is individually demanded by three very different theories of distributive justice.

The implication of this theoretical convergence is that the processes of executive selection and compensation should occupy a focal area for governance scholars and those concerned with the ethics of executive compensation. For such scholars, a thorough examination of executive selection and compensation *processes* represents a productive course of future research that may lead to a better understanding of how these processes can be improved and made more transparent and open. This may ultimately pave the way to the establishment of consistently appropriate and ethically sound executive compensation arrangements.

ACKNOWLEDGMENTS

I am grateful to Sarah Holtman for her general insights on distributive justice theory, to Christopher Moore for detailed and helpful conceptual comments during the initial development of these ideas, to David Souder for valuable feedback and countless discussions on the topic, and to Norm Bowie for comments on an early draft. Special thanks for specific feedback from Rob Phillips, Lyla Hamilton, the participants at the 2004 Japha Symposium sponsored by the University of Colorado, and the participants at the 2005 Markkula Global Conference on Business Ethics sponsored by Santa Clara University.

REFERENCES

Bavaria, S. 1991. Corporate ethics should start in the boardroom. *Business Horizons*, **34**(1): 9–12.

Bebchuk, L. A. and Fried, J. M. 2003. Executive compensation as an agency problem. *Journal of Economic Perspectives*, **17**(3): 71–92.

Blasi, J. R. and Kruse, D. L. 2003. *In the Company of Owners: The Truth About Stock Options and Why Every Employee Should Have Them*. New York: Basic Books.

Brin, D. W. 2002. Exit strategy: directors are starting to rethink lucrative severance payouts they give to fired CEOs. *Wall Street Journal*. April 12, R15, New York.

Chung, K. and Charoenwong, C. 1991. Investment options, assets in place and the risk of stocks. *Financial Management*, **20**(3): 21–33.

Ciulla, J. 2000. *The Working Life*. New York: Random House Times Books.

Conyon, M. J. and Peck, S. I. 1998. Board control, remuneration committees, and top management compensation. *Academy of Management Journal*, **41**(2): 146–157.

Davis, G. F., Yoo, M., and Baker, W. E. 2003. The small world of the American corporate elite, 1982–2001. *Strategic Organization*, **1**(3): 301–326.

Dworkin, R. 2000. *Sovereign Virtue*. Cambridge, MA: Harvard University Press.

Farkas, S., Duffett, A., Johnson, J., and Syat, B. 2004. A few bad apples? An exploratory look at what typical Americans think about business ethics today. A report for the Kettering Foundation from Public Agenda, available at http://www.publicagenda.org. Last accessed on June 29, 2005.

Freeman, R. E. 1984. *Strategic Management: A Stakeholder Approach*. Boston, MA: Pittman.

Friedman, M. 1970. The social responsibility of business is to increase its profits. *The New York Times Magazine*, **33**: 122–126.

Hall, B. J. and Murphy, K. J. 2003. The trouble with stock options. *Journal of Economic Perspectives*, **17**(3): 49–70.

Harris, J. and Bromiley, P. 2003. *Incentives to Cheat: Executive Compensation and Corporate Malfeasance*. Paper presented at the 2003 Strategic Management Society International Conference, Baltimore, MD.

Hayward, M. L. A., Rindova, V. P., and Pollock, T. G. 2004. Believing one's own press: the causes and consequences of CEO celebrity. *Strategic Management Journal*, **25**(7): 637–653.

Henderson, A. D. and Fredrickson, J. W. 1996. Information-processing demands as a determinant of CEO compensation. *Academy of Management Journal*, **39**(3): 575–607.

Jensen, M. C. 2002. Value maximization, stakeholder theory, and the corporate objective function. *Business Ethics Quarterly*, **12**(2): 235–256.

Jensen, M. C. and Meckling, W. 1976. Theory of the firm: managerial behavior, agency costs and ownership structure. *Journal of Financial Economics*, **3**: 305–360.

Jensen, M. C. and Murphy, K. J. 1990. CEO incentives – It's not how much you pay, but how. *Harvard Business Review*, **68**(3): 138–149.

Lublin, J. 1996. The great divide. *Wall Street Journal*, April 11, New York.

Lublin, J. S. and Hechinger, J. 2002. Forced exits can pay richly for some CEOs. *Wall Street Journal*, June 5, New York.

Meyers, M. 2003. Economists debate the role of technology in '90s boom. *Star Tribune*, January 4, Minneapolis, MN.

Mishra, C. S., McConaughy, D. L., and Gobeli, D. H. 2000. Effectiveness of CEO pay-for-performance. *Review of Financial Economics*, **9**: 1–13.

Monks, R. A. G. and Minow, N. 2004. *Corporate Governance*, 3rd edn. Malden, MA: Blackwell.

Murphy, K. J. 1999. Executive compensation. In O. Ashenfelter and D. Card, eds., *Handbook of Labour Economics*. Amsterdam: Elsevier, pp. 2485–2563.

Nichols, D. and Subramaniam, C. 2001. Executive compensation: excessive or equitable? *Journal of Business Ethics*, 29: 339–351.

Nozick, R. 1974. *Anarchy, State, and Utopia*. New York: Basic Books.

Nussbaum, M. C. 2000. *Women and Human Development: The Capabilities Approach*. New York: Cambridge University Press.

O'Connor, J. P., Priem, R. L., Coombs, J. E., and Gilley, K. M. 2003. Do CEO stock options prevent or promote corporate accounting irregularities? *Working paper, University of Wisconsin, Milwaukee, WI*.

Patton, A. 1951. Incentive compensation for executives. *Harvard Business Review*, 29(5): 35–47.

Phillips, R. 2003. *Stakeholder Theory and Organizational Ethics*. San Francisco, CA: Berrett-Koehler Publishers, Inc.

Porac, J., Wade, J., and Pollock, T. G. 1999. Industry categories and the politics of the comparable firm in CEO compensation. *Administrative Science Quarterly*, 44: 112–144.

Rawls, J. 1971. *A Theory of Justice*. Cambridge, MA: Harvard University Press.

Rosen, S. 1981. The economics of superstars. *American Economic Review*, 71: 845–858.

Rynes, S. L. and Gerhart, B. 2000. *Compensation in Organizations: Current Research and Practice*. San Francisco, CA: Jossey-Bass.

Schnatterly, K. 2003. Increasing firm value through detection and prevention of white-collar crime. *Strategic Management Journal*, 24: 587–614.

Sen, A. 1997. Economics, business principles, and moral sentiments. *Business Ethics Quarterly*, 7(3): 5–15.

Sen, A. 1999. *Development as Freedom*. New York: Knopf.

Staw, B. M. and Epstein, L. D. 2000. What bandwagons bring: effects of popular management techniques on corporate performance, reputation, and CEO pay. *Administrative Science Quarterly*, 45: 523–556.

Surowiecki, J. 2003. The financial page: the coup de Grasso. *New Yorker*, October 6.

Thomas, L. 2004. Saying Grasso duped big Board, suit seeks return of $100 million, *New York Times*, May 25.

Useem, J. 2003. Have they no shame? *Fortune*, April 28, 147: 56–64.

Varian, H. R. 2002. Economic scene. *New York Times*, March 14.

Werhane, P. H. and Radin, T. J. 2004. *Employment and Employee Rights*. Malden, MA: Blackwell Publishing.

Westphal, J. D. and Khanna, P. 2003. Keeping directors in line: social distancing as a control mechanism in the corporate elite. *Administrative Science Quarterly*, 48: 361–398.

Yermack, D. 2004. Flights of fancy: corporate jets, CEO perquisites, and inferior shareholder returns. *Working paper, Stern School of Business, New York University*.

Young, C. 1998. Trends in executive compensation. *Journal of Business Strategy*, 19(2): 21–24.

Young, M. N. and Buchholtz, A. K. 2002. Firm performance and CEO pay: relational demography as a moderator. *Journal of Managerial Issues*, 14(3): 296–313.

5

Justice, Incentives, and Executive Compensation

William H. Shaw
Professor of Philosophy, Department of Philosophy, San Jose State University

There are various possible ways of defending inequality of income, in general, and high levels of executive compensation, in particular, as just, fair, or morally acceptable. One of the most important of these is the *incentives argument*, which finds widespread favor both in popular discourse and among moral philosophers and other academics. It contends that society justly permits those with special talents to receive extra, equality-undermining income, when doing so is necessary to entice them to apply themselves to certain tasks that only they can do or that they can do better than others. In this chapter, I examine the incentives argument from the perspective of three leading theories of distributive justice – utilitarianism, libertarianism, and Rawlsian egalitarianism – probing the argument's assumptions and limitations with respect to the question of executive compensation. Although each of these theories appears to support the incentives argument, closer inspection shows the difficulties of squaring it with any of them.

The Incentives Argument

The incentives argument, as I have stated it, is general in scope, but the focus of this chapter is the financial remuneration of CEOs and other leading corporate executives. When I refer to the incentives argument, then, I shall have in mind specifically the incentives argument for high levels of executive compensation. For convenience, I refer to the CEOs and other corporate executives who are my concern as "the Talented." By this, I mean those talented in business, that is, those men and women who have special business competence, managerial abilities, entrepreneurial instincts, leadership skills, or other traits that can be valuable to the firm or corporation employing them, but that are in short supply and that most other employees or potential employees lack. Calling them "the Talented" might be thought to prejudice the question in favor of the incentives argument or even to disparage those supposed by it to be less talented. However, for my critical purposes, it does no harm to present the incentives argument in its own terms. The incentives argument assumes that in the business world there are inevitably certain individuals – the Talented – who are well placed in the employment market because of their particular skills and abilities. These individuals command high salaries; they have a choice of lucrative job opportunities; and they can work more or less hard, adjusting their productivity according to the remuneration they receive. The incentives argument takes the existence of the Talented for granted, but they are only assumed to be talented in this special sense. Other people may have talents, skills, and personal traits that are more valuable in other ways, but that benefit them less in the marketplace.

The incentives argument asserts, then, that it is just to pay the Talented significantly more than others get paid, either inside or outside the firm, in order to induce them to undertake certain tasks for which they, because of their special abilities, are better suited than others, and to apply themselves diligently to those tasks. It is a moral argument, of course, but it is not a desert-based argument. It does not claim that the Talented deserve moral credit for their particular abilities, nor does it contend that the talents in question inherently merit superior reward. Perhaps, both propositions are true, but that is not what the incentives argument is asserting. It is a market-oriented argument. If the talents in question were not in short supply, the incentives argument would not support high compensation for the possessors of those talents.

The incentives argument should be distinguished from two other arguments in favor of paying some people incomes that are significantly greater than what most others earn. First, one might maintain that it is just to pay higher salaries to those who have forgone income or made other sacrifices to acquire the skills or experience necessary for certain jobs, for example, by passing up gainful employment in order to undergo arduous training, ill-paid apprenticeship, or advanced study. Simple fairness, it might be argued, requires that those who have undergone specialized training at some cost to themselves should subsequently earn more than those who chose not to exert themselves to acquire those talents. Second, one might urge paying some people extra to reimburse them for current sacrifices, such as long hours, hard work, or the responsibilities they have undertaken. These two arguments may well provide morally respectable grounds for one's receiving higher than average pay, but they are distinct from the incentives argument. The incentives argument does not assert that justice requires high compensation for the Talented because of their past sacrifices or present exertions.

Although granting people additional compensation because of past sacrifices or present exertions produces an unequal distribution of current income, it tends to promote equality of welfare. This is because recompensing people for extra efforts tends "to make the total prospects of different persons equal" (Brandt, 1979). Following up on this thought, we can distinguish between payments necessary to offset the welfare losses that one would otherwise incur by undertaking a certain job or pursuing a certain career and payments that reward people above and beyond that level. The incentives argument focuses only on the latter, on what we might call "pure incentives." It assumes that the motivational structure of people in our society (if not everywhere) is such that the prospect of income above and beyond what others earn, and beyond what is required to equalize people's bene-fits and gains across their lifetimes, is generally or, at least, frequently needed to entice those with special talents to apply themselves to those tasks that they can do better than others. In order to elicit the efforts of the Talented, therefore, higher than average pay is both necessary and just.

The Incentives Argument in a Rawlsian Framework

Rawls's theory of justice provides a normative framework capable of supporting the incentives argument. Although his theory is egalitarian in its overall thrust, his famous difference principle permits social and economic inequalities insofar as they work to the benefit of the least advantaged members of society. Rawls does not assert that the least well-off always benefit from economic inequality, that the gains of the better-off inevitably trickle down to the poor, or that income inequality invariably creates a larger social pie to be shared by everyone. Rather, his point is that social justice does not demand equality at any price. Still, the dif-ference principle lays down a stringent standard. To be justified, inequalities must not merely benefit people on average; they must benefit the least advantaged. And they must not merely benefit them; they must work to their greatest expected benefit – in other words, they must make the least well-off better-off than they would be under any other system of reward and distribution. More specifically, then, Rawls's theory holds that inequalities are justified only if, and just to the extent that, permitting some people to be better-off than average results in the least well-off segment of society being better-off than it would have been under a strictly equal division of social and economic benefits and burdens.

Rawls's difference principle seems to accommodate, even invite, the incentives argument. Nevertheless, to succeed, a Rawlsian-based incentives argument must clear a high bar. Any such argument must show, of course, that paying the Talented handsomely really does work to the greatest expected benefit of the least advantaged. This in turn presumably requires establishing (1) that such compensation is indeed necessary to induce the Talented to undertake work that they would otherwise decline and (2) that their incentive-induced labors increase the resources that society has at its disposal in such ways and to such an extent that no alternative system of economic distribution and reward could have benefited more the least well-off segment of society. These are large empirical claims, and the burden of proof clearly falls on the proponent of the incentives argument, because for Rawls equality is the default norm: it is deviations from that norm that require justification. On the other hand, the proponent of the incentives argument needs to initially establish only a rough generalization, not a universal truth, namely, that a system of economic organization that permits pure incentive pay tends to work better than any other system does, as judged from the perspective of the least advantaged.

Let us suppose that one can support this generalization. Other questions then arise. In particular, exactly how much of an incentive do the Talented need, and how much do the least advantaged benefit from rewarding the Talented at various monetary levels? Presumably, two opposing tendencies are at work. On the one hand, the greater the incentive, the greater the effort called forth; on the other, the greater the rewards to the Talented, the fewer are the resources, at least initially, for society to expend directly and immediately for the benefit of the least advantaged. Having assumed the general legitimacy of incentives from a Rawlsian point of view, we thus encounter at the level of policy implementation even more daunting empirical issues. And yet these issues are absolutely central to the real world. In 1980, *Fortune* 500 CEOs earned on average about 40 times what those working for them received; 20 years later they earned more than 400 times as much, and they are estimated to have earned 530 times as much last year (*Financial Times*, 2004). How plausible is it to suppose that the least advantaged have benefited more from policies permitting this vast increase in CEO wealth than they would have from any alternative set of policies? Like me, you may have a strong hunch what the answer to that question is, but rigorously establishing that hunch may not be so easy. Bear in mind, though, that it is departures from equality that need to be justified, and the greater the incentive-based inequalities one is seeking to legitimate, the higher will be the standard of evidence that one will have to meet. Even if one can, in principle, square the incentives argument with Rawls's theory, the difficulty of doing so grows exponentially as the proposed payments to the Talented increase.

Rawls's principles of justice are intended to govern the basic structure of society and set the framework for assessing socioeconomic policy and related institutional arrangements. He is unconcerned, at least in the first instance, with the justice or injustice of particular transactions, viewed in isolation. This fact raises the problem of how to live by Rawlsian principles in a non-Rawlsian world. Suppose that the board of directors of World Widgets Incorporated accepts Rawls's theory, believing that a just society would operate according to his principles, how is the board to proceed? Specifically, should it approve incentive pay to the Talented, and if so, how much? According to Rawls, the board, like other members of society, has a natural duty to help establish and sustain just socioeconomic arrangements, but unfortunately this gives the board little guidance with regard to executive compensation, and it's unclear to me how exactly it is to proceed.

Things may be different with respect to the Talented, though. It can be argued that if they accept Rawls's theory – in particular, if they believe that socioeconomic inequalities are justified only to the extent necessary to maximally benefit the least advantaged – then they should be willing to work without pure incentive pay (Cohen, 2000). In *A Theory of Justice*, Rawls writes, "Human beings have a desire to express their nature as free and equal moral persons, and this they do most adequately by acting from the principles that they would acknowledge in the original position" (Rawls, 1971: 528). But if the Talented embrace the difference principle, how can they demand special compensation for utilizing their talents, compensation that goes beyond whatever is necessary to make up for the strain or unpleasantness of their work or for the sacrifices they underwent to acquire those talents? The Talented cannot plausibly claim that their receiving this compensation is genuinely necessary to enhance the position of the least advantaged because it is the Talented themselves who have chosen to make their receiving it necessary. It is not that the Talented cannot perform the work for which they are better suited than others without this compensation, but that they decline to do so. Exploiting one's advantaged position in this way seems incompatible with being sincerely and robustly committed to the difference principle.

The argument I have just advanced makes it unclear whether we are talking about a Rawlsian or a non-Rawlsian world. If we assume a Rawlsian world, that is, a world guided by his principles and in which people have a developed sense of justice, then the argument seems convincing that the difference principle would permit far less inequality than Rawls and others may assume. But what if the

Talented, like the board of World Widgets, accepts Rawls's theory but lives in a non-Rawlsian world? Is their insisting on high compensation compatible with "acting from the principles that they would acknowledge in the original position"? These questions raise issues that are too complicated to explore fully here. But it does seem that a case can be made that those who embrace Rawls's theory should endeavor to live up to its spirit even in an unjust society. In such circumstances, perhaps, the most Rawlsian course of conduct might be for the Talented to accept the high pay to which a less than fully just system entitles them but to expend the purely incentive portion of that pay in ways that improve the lot of the least well-off. On the other hand, it is even less certain what Rawls's theory implies for those talented denizens of a non-Rawlsian world who do not accept Rawls's theory.

Incentives and the Promotion of Social Well-Being

Let us leave these Rawlsian perplexities aside, however, and turn to the utilitarian approach to distributive justice, which appears even more hospitable to the incentives argument than Rawls's theory does. Here, it is a good idea to begin with John Stuart Mill, whose account of justice well represents, I think, mainstream utilitarian thinking. Mill writes, "Justice is a name for certain classes of moral rules which concern the essentials of human well-being more nearly, and are therefore of more absolute obligation, than any other rules for the guidance of life" (Mill, 1957: 73). Although for utilitarians like Mill justice is ultimately a matter of promoting social well-being, not every issue of social utility is a matter of justice. The concept of justice identifies certain important social utilities, that is, certain rules or rights, the upholding of which is crucial for human flourishing. Justice is not an independent moral standard, distinct from the general utilitarian principle. Rather, the maximization of happiness ultimately determines what is just and unjust.

Mill goes on to argue that only utilitarianism can provide a determinate standard of justice. Otherwise, one is always left with a plethora of competing principles, all of which have some plausibility but which are mutually incompatible. As an example, he points to the conflict between rival principles of justice that occurs when one asks whether it is just that more talented workers should receive greater remuneration than less talented workers. Mill spells out both sides to the issue, showing how each appeals to a very plausible principle of justice. "Justice," he writes, "has in this case two sides to it, which it is impossible to bring into harmony, and the two disputants have chosen opposite sides; the one looks to what it is just that the individual should receive, the other to what it is just that the community should give." Each disputant is, from his or her own point of view, unanswerable. "Any choice between them, on grounds of justice," Mill continues, "must be perfectly arbitrary." What, then, is the answer? For Mill, the utilitarian, it is straightforward: "Social utility alone can decide the preference" (1957: 71).

This perspective naturally guides utilitarians in their approach to the incentives argument, and the question for them is whether a system of socioeconomic policies and institutional arrangements that underwrite high compensation for the Talented will produce better long-term results than any other system would. The word *underwrite* in the last sentence is ambiguous, and sorting out this ambiguity is part of the challenge facing utilitarians. Is copious compensation for the Talented to be legally permitted or not? If permissible, is it to be encouraged or discouraged, and in what ways and to what extent? Assuming incentive pay is to be encouraged or at least not actively discouraged, at what rate is it to be taxed? This is an exceedingly important question, for much of the incentive benefit, real or imagined, from high executive compensation can be retained even if it is heavily taxed.

Consider, for example, this exchange a few years ago between a *New York Times* reporter and L. Dennis Kozlowski, the then CEO of Tyco International:

> *Question*: It's often said that at a certain level it no longer matters how much any of you make, that you would be doing just as good a job for $100 million less or $20 million less.
>
> *Kozlowski*: Yeah, all my meals are paid for, for as long as I'm around. So, I'm not working for that any longer. But it does make a difference in the charities I ultimately leave monies behind to, and it's a way of keeping score. (Quoted in Isbister, 2001)

But to the extent that high levels of compensation are necessary to motivate the Talented because they are a good way of keeping score, that desideratum can be achieved even if government eventually taxes this money away. Presumably, CEOs like Kozlowski keep score by comparing total corporate compensation, not income tax returns.

In addressing these issues, utilitarians face the same difficult but important empirical questions that Rawlsians do, but with two shifts of emphasis. First, their theory makes the point of reference the benefits received by the average individual, not the benefits received by the least well-off members of society.

The utilitarian goal is a system that maximizes benefit, rather than, as Rawls would have it, "maximins" it. Second, the utilitarian understanding of benefit – namely, happiness or well-being – is broader than the Rawlsian metric of "primary social goods," which consists chiefly of "rights and liberties, opportunities and powers, income and wealth" (Rawls, 1971: 62, 92). That metric may be more manageable than the utilitarian notion of well-being, over the interpretation of which utilitarians themselves disagree, but it is hard to doubt that people's well-being can be affected by factors other than the primary goods they receive. Insofar as incentive pay influences or is influenced by these factors, utilitarianism will take them into account. Our competitive urges and our desire for social status might be among such factors, as would, perhaps, our need for social solidarity, our leveling instincts, and our feelings of envy.

In general, however, a utilitarian-based incentives argument faces empirical issues very similar to those that a Rawlsian argument must address. Do policies and institutional structures permitting or encouraging superior compensation for the Talented benefit society as a whole more than would alternative socioeconomic arrangements and, if they do, what limits, if any, should be placed on income inequality? In *Laws*, Book V, Plato argues that for the well-being of society the Talented should ideally have no more than four times the wealth of their neighbors. Would keeping income inequality within a ratio of 4 : 1 be optimal, or would 40 : 1 or 400 : 1 be better? This question eludes easy answer, but several considerations reduce the likelihood that utilitarians will routinely authorize rewarding the Talented anywhere near as bountifully as they are today.

First, many of the Talented possess their socially useful but relatively scarce talents, not because of innate ability alone, but also because of the comparative advantages they enjoyed in education, upbringing, and social environment. A society committed, as a utilitarian society would be, to substantive (as opposed to merely formal) equality of opportunity would find itself with a larger pool of talented or potentially talented citizens, thus reducing the ability of the Talented successfully to demand extremely high levels of compensation. Although it pertains less directly to the Talented in business, utilitarians will, as a related matter, seek also to dismantle any restrictions on entry into an occupational field, the primary purpose of which is to buoy the incomes of those in that field.

A second consideration is that jobs that only the Talented can perform, or that they can perform better than others, tend to be more intrinsically engaging and rewarding, in large measure because they permit greater autonomy and involve a greater exercise of skill, judgment, and expertise. They also typically bring greater social prestige. Imagine, for the sake of argument, that a CEO's working hours were only as long, and only as grueling, as those of your average cubicle dweller. Under these circumstances, it is hard to imagine that people with the temperament and talent for being corporate leaders would prefer to be cubicle dwellers instead and that only the lure of high compensation can draw them out of their stalls and into the boardroom.

Third, society has strong utilitarian grounds for resisting demands from the Talented for high compensation, even if acceding to them seems expedient at the time. Arguably, society will be better-off in the long run to the extent that it discourages the Talented from seeking compensation that is out of all proportion to what others receive. In addition to worrying about the economic cost, utilitarians will resist establishing norms that reinforce people's greedy instincts. They will not want avarice to become accepted, let alone esteemed and respected, as a legitimate human motivation. Rather, they will try, at least to a moderate extent, to discourage people's purely selfish motivations and to reinforce their more altruistic and socially harmonious instincts. In addition, the diminishing marginal utility of money provides independent utilitarian grounds for inclining away from extreme inequalities of income.

Thus, various considerations of long-run social welfare, both economic and noneconomic, favor promoting social norms that reprove extreme inequalities of income and that reinforce job-related motivational considerations other than the desire for a disproportionately high monetary reward. Moreover, we all know that money does not necessarily bring happiness, a fact confirmed by social psychologists, who report that Americans, Europeans, and Japanese are no more pleased with their lives now than they were in the 1950s despite the very substantial increase in standard of living that all these societies have enjoyed (Diener et al., 1999; Easterlin, 2004; Frank, 2004). For this reason, too, utilitarians will be reluctant to risk sacrificing other social goods by promoting or sustaining extreme income disparities in a somewhat speculative effort to increase the GDP marginally.

These ruminations are far from conclusive, but they do suggest that although utilitarians are in principle open to the incentives argument, they will view it skeptically. By contrast with Rawls, for whom equal distribution is the baseline against which any proposed inequalities must be justified, utilitarianism is, in the abstract, indifferent between equality and inequality. However, for the reasons I have given, utilitarians will in fact be reluctant, I believe, to countenance extreme inequality of income and disinclined, in particular, toward huge monetary bonuses for the Talented, thus shifting the burden of proof onto the proponent of the incentives argument.

These broad and somewhat tentative remarks concern the utilitarian perspective on distributive justice, that is, on the rules and principles that should, on grounds of utility, structure a society's socioeconomic institutions and guide its fundamental policies. But suppose, as seems likely, that utilitarians will favor economic arrangements that limit economic inequality and keep executive compensation within more modest bounds than we see today, what does this mean for the board of directors at World Widgets and for the Talented themselves, who are positioned in the real world successfully to insist upon compensation well beyond what utilitarians are likely to approve? What does a utilitarian approach to economic justice, in general, and the incentives argument, in particular, imply for their conduct?

As with Rawls, here one finds some uncertainty internal to the theory depending on whether one focuses on individual conduct or on the rules that are to govern society's basic socioeconomic structure. In particular, there is a tension within utilitarianism between the goal of always acting so as to maximize utility and the goal of instilling in people a firm disposition to follow certain secondary moral rules, among which are the rules that define justice – rules that are necessary to guide and coordinate people's conduct in ways that maximize happiness on balance and in the long run. This raises a host of complicated and contested issues, but exploring them here would take us too far afield. Still, one can safely say that the board of World Widgets, if it is utilitarian in its orientation, will take into account how its decisions about corporate compensation help move society closer to, or further from, the socioeconomic norms to which utilitarians would want society to adhere. The Talented too, if they are utilitarian, will take this into consideration. Moreover, as utilitarians they will desire to be, or to become, people with wide and deep sympathy for the well-being of others, people whose own material self-interest is not the overriding goal of their lives.

However, let us now turn to our third theory of justice.

Libertarianism and the Market for Talent

Advancing the incentives argument from within a libertarian framework appears to spare one from having to make the difficult empirical case that both Rawls and utilitarianism require one to make. Libertarians are dubious of the very concept of *social* justice if that concept is taken to designate some overarching standard to which the distribution of socioeconomic benefits and burdens must correspond. Libertarians reject, in Robert Nozick's words, end-state or patterned principles of justice. Rather, things are justly distributed just to the extent that people are entitled to the holdings they possess; people are entitled to their holdings (i.e., to their money, property, and other goods) as long as they have acquired them fairly; and people have acquired their holdings fairly if they have done so without violating anyone's basic rights – in particular, if they have obtained them through voluntary exchange without force or fraud.

With regard to the incentives argument, libertarianism implies that high pay for the Talented is just if and only if all parties have freely agreed to it. If a firm chooses to remunerate handsomely certain key individuals, then that is its business and no one else's. How the company spends its own money is up to it; no one can criticize it on grounds of justice for supposedly paying some employees too much or other employees too little as long as those employees freely accepted the terms of their employment. Presumably, any company pays its employees what it does because this is what the market requires it to pay for people with those particular talents and because the firm has determined that it is worth its while to spend the money to acquire those talents. If the market dictates that a seasoned Chartered Financial Analyst (CFA) costs, say, $1.3 million in salary, stock options, and other forms of compensation, and the company judges that he or she is worth it, then from a libertarian perspective, that should settle the matter.

Here, however, the proponent of the incentives argument shifts ground slightly. Libertarianism does not assume that high pay for the Talented is necessary in the sense that without such compensation the Talented will inevitably decline to perform the type of work in question and undertake instead labor of an altogether different sort. Rather, libertarianism simply accepts the fact that talent is scarce and that the marketplace bids up the price of scarce but valuable resources. It has no problem granting that, because their skills are scarce, the Talented might successfully demand and receive, say, $2X or $3X for doing work of a certain sort even though they would be happy to work for $1X in the sense that they would prefer to do the work in question for that sum than perform work of a different kind. Compensation that is significantly higher than what one would be willing to accept for work of a certain sort might be called "employment rent." In the simple textbook world of introductory economics, high wages for a particular set of talents should, of course, call forth a greater supply, a decline in compensation for those who possess those talents, and an ultimate balancing of supply and demand – unless, of course, this is impossible because the particular talent, like hitting 60 major-league home runs a season, is in inherently short supply, at least in the short to medium term.

From a libertarian perspective, of course, this is irrelevant. If you want a home-run hitter, then you must pay the hitter a salary he will accept, and if his talents are in short supply and there are other bidders, it will cost you more.

But suppose the potential supply of home-run hitters is not really all that short; perhaps, if you advertised in China, you would find plenty of them. This, too, would seem to be irrelevant from a libertarian point of view. Exchanges must be free and fair, that is all. The market helps to explain why people pay what they do, but libertarian theory does not require us to be rational economic agents; we are free to give gifts, pay above market prices for things, and spend our funds imprudently if that is what we choose to do. But while this is not a problem for libertarianism in general, it becomes one when we focus on publicly traded corporations, the directors of which have fiduciary responsibilities to the company's stockholders, responsibilities that arise from the firm's having sold shares to investors. The board of directors of World Widgets cannot justly give away corporate assets, spend stockholder money foolishly, or pay above market wages to the Talented.

Within a libertarian framework, a publicly held firm acts unfairly if it hires people it does not need or pays them more than the market requires or more than the value they are likely to create for the company. The firm's responsibilities to its stockholder do not mandate that it always behave in economically optimal ways, that is, that it always succeed in maximizing profits and enhancing shareholder value. That is difficult to do. But the firm and its directors are required to make a good faith effort to do so. If a board of directors uses the incentives argument to justify paying the Talented superior compensation without inquiring whether equivalent skills might be obtained at a lower price, it fails in its responsibilities to shareholders. This is especially true if, in effect, it delegates responsibility back to management to determine its own compensation. If the firm squanders its money on the Talented, then this is a kind of fraud against shareholders, which libertarianism forbids (unless, of course, potential shareholders are told ahead of time, as are the stockholders of the Green Bay Packers, that they are not investing in a profit-making enterprise).

So, a libertarian approach to the incentives argument cannot, after all, avoid addressing some challenging empirical issues. Are the skills of the Talented as scarce as they are assumed to be? Could equivalent skills be had for less money by hiring inside the firm or by recruiting executives from Japan, Germany, Britain, or India? Could those talents be had for less by allowing candidates to bid against one another by offering to undertake the job in question for a lower salary than their competitors? To a board of directors immersed in the real world, these questions might seem feckless and unfruitful, but they raise a genuine challenge, for the studies all show that there is no correlation – except possibly a negative one – between high CEO pay and corporate performance (*Financial Times*, 2004).

For a libertarian-based incentives argument, moreover, these are not simply intriguing factual questions, the answers to which are irrelevant to what a firm has a right to do. Libertarianism focuses our attention on the justice of individual transactions, which includes the question of whether a company is fulfilling the agreement it has with stockholders. It is no response to say that unhappy stockholders are free to sell their shares in companies with profligate boards. Of course, they are. If after shopping around you choose to buy a television set from me, but later decide that you are unhappy with it or that it is not providing the benefits you had hoped for, then you have no complaint against me. You can sell it to someone else or give it away. But if I misrepresented the product I sold you, then it is no response to say that if you are unhappy with it, then you can sell it to someone else.

Who has the burden of proof in determining whether a particular firm is acting justly to stockholders in paying what it does for talent? Libertarian justice requires that a company make at least a good-faith effort to fulfill its responsibilities to stockholders. And the burden of establishing that such an effort has been made can only fall on the board of directors. Both full disclosure of its compensation policies and of its procedures for recruiting top executives and an open discussion with shareholders of the principles underlying those policies and procedures would seem to be necessary prerequisites for a company to establish that it is sincerely endeavoring to meet its fiduciary responsibilities.

Conclusion

Despite its being incomplete and somewhat open ended, we must now conclude our survey of what these three theories have to say about the incentives argument. This widely accepted argument, you will recall, maintains that high executive compensation is just because it is necessary to entice those with special talents in business to undertake work for which they are better suited than others. Our survey was undertaken in the belief that assessment of this argument must inevitably presuppose some theory or foundational principles of distributive justice and that, in the absence of a philosophical consensus about which theories or principles are best, there is no better place to begin than with these three exceedingly influential contemporary theories of economic justice. The incentives argument can, with some plausibility, be advanced within the framework of each of these theories. But despite, or perhaps because of, the various empirical uncertainties and unanswered questions we have encountered, we have seen that, from whichever of these perspectives we choose to take up, sustaining the incentives argument and marshalling a compelling case for high executive compensation on this basis turns out to be a more difficult and challenging project than many suspect, a project that only becomes more daunting, the higher the level of compensation that one is proposing to justify.

REFERENCES

Brandt, Richard B. 1979. *A Theory of the Good and the Right*. Oxford: Oxford University Press, p. 320.

Cohen, G. A. 2000. *If You're an Egalitarian, How Come You're So Rich?* Cambridge, MA: Harvard University Press, pp. 126–127.

Diener, Ed., Suh, Eunkook M., Lucas, Richard E., and Smith, Heidi L. 1999. Subjective well-being: three decades of progress. *Psychological Bulletin*, 125(2): 288.

Easterlin, Richard A. 2004. The economics of happiness. *Daedalus*, Spring: 31.

Financial Times. 2004. Off the leash: what will bring executive pay under control? August 24, p. 11.

Frank, Robert H. 2004. How not to buy happiness. *Daedalus*, Spring: 70.

Isbister, John. 2001. *Capitalism and Justice*. Bloomfield, CT: Kumarian Press, p. 63.

Mill, John Stuart. 1957. *Utilitarianism*. Indianapolis, IN: Bobbs-Merrill, p. 73

Rawls, John. 1971. *A Theory of Justice*. Cambridge, MA: Harvard University Press, p. 528.

6

CEO Compensation and Virtue Ethics

Michael Potts
Associate Professor of Philosophy, Chair, Department of Philosophy and Religion,
Methodist College, 5400 Ramsey Street, Fayetteville, NC 28311-1498

Introduction

In this chapter, I argue that the debate over the fairness of executive pay is not to
be settled by a simple examination of earnings. Using the Aristotelian virtue-
oriented approach to ethics, applied to business ethics by Robert Solomon,
I argue that business is primarily a practice, a community of individuals engaged
in a cooperative endeavor to deliver goods and services for the good of society. As
such, certain virtues, such as integrity, moral courage, and justice, are essential to
the practice of business. I then argue that justice in pay implies that more modest
executive pay – across the board, regardless of company profitability – is the just
option for the practice of business. Finally, I discuss the advantages of the virtue
approach applied to the issue of CEO compensation as opposed to utilitarian and
deontological approaches.

The debate over the fairness of executive compensation, once limited to corporate
boardrooms, has recently become important to the general public, with media
outlets reporting widespread public resentment over rapid increases in pay for
top executives, increases that often seem to occur regardless of company profitability. The gap between the pay of top executives and the average company
employee has fed the continuing controversy, as have the "perks," such as stock
options, travel, security, and housing, often included in executive compensation
packages. There is a growing perception that current levels of compensation for
executives, particularly CEOs, are no longer "fair." *Business Week's* annual special
report on executive pay notes that the top 25 CEOs had an average annual pay of
$32.7 million, "more than 900 times the annual salary of the typical U.S. worker"
(Lavelle et al., 2004). In an era in which many companies are cutting costs by
laying off employees, such compensation seems to many to be unjust. But determining what level of compensation is unjust is a difficult task. Elaine Sternberg

believes that such "inequalities between workers and executives . . . are . . . irrelevant to the ethics of executive remuneration." She further claims that "[t]he sole principle that should govern the allocation of rewards within the ethical business or corporation is distributive justice: remuneration and responsibilities and honors should be proportional to contributions to the business or corporate end." She has in mind "contributions to long-term owner value," so that "the executive whose remuneration increases while the value of the company he manages declines, is indeed being rewarded unfairly" (Sternberg, 2000: 216).

What is fair when it comes to executive pay? Is the current high-level compensation of top executives, in particular CEOs, a form of injustice? It seems unjust to compensate a CEO with a $10 million annual package when a company is losing money. But when a company is successful due, at least in part, to a skilled CEO, is it a moral fault to compensate that CEO accordingly? Colgate-Palmolive Co's CEO Reuben Mark was recently given "4 million split-adjusted options . . . that would pay off only if Colgate stock surged as much as 80%." It rose "286% over 10 years," and Mr Mark cashed in "the options that made up most of his $141.1 million pay package" (Lavelle et al., 2004). Was this fair compensation for a job well done, or was it excessive? In this chapter, I will argue that the debate over the fairness of executive pay is not to be settled by a simple examination of earnings. Using the Aristotelian virtue-oriented approach to ethics, applied to business ethics by Robert Solomon, I shall argue that business is primarily a practice, a community of individuals engaged in a cooperative endeavor to deliver goods and services for the good of society. As such, certain virtues, such as integrity, moral courage, and justice, are essential to the practice of business. I shall then argue that justice in pay implies that more modest executive pay – across the board, regardless of company profitability – is the just option for the practice of business.

What is a Practice?

Alasdair MacIntyre develops the notion of a "practice" in his influential book, *After Virtue* (1984). He defines a "practice" as follows:

> any coherent and complex form of socially established cooperative human activity through which goods internal to that form of activity are realized in the course of trying to achieve those standards of excellence which are appropriate to, and partially definitive of, that form or activity, with the result that human powers to achieve excellence, and human conceptions of the ends and goods involved, are systematically extended. (1984: 187)

MacIntyre gives several examples of such activities, such as chess, farming, physics, the historian's work, and painting. But more important than these particular practices is "the creation and sustaining of human communities – of households, cities, [and] nations . . ." (MacIntyre, 1984: 187–188).

MacIntyre distinguishes between "goods external" and "goods internal" to a particular practice. Using medicine as an example, there are a number of "goods external" to the practice of medicine, such as money and elevated social status. A "good internal" to the practice of medicine is helping a sick person in need. Since this good is partly constitutive of the practice of medicine, the standards of excellence required for fulfilling that good are found *within* the practice of medicine. Thus, "A practice involves standards of excellence and obedience to rules as well as the achievement of goods. To enter into a practice is to accept the authority of those standards and the inadequacy of my own performance as judged by them" (MacIntyre, 1984: 190). Although standards are not sacrosanct and can be revised, "we cannot be initiated into a practice without accepting the authority of the best standards realized so far" (MacIntyre, 1984: 190). These standards are not subjective or arbitrary, since they stem from the internal goods of the practice itself.

Unlike external goods, of which some members of the community have more than others, gaining internal goods "is a good for the whole community who participate in the practice" (MacIntyre, 1984: 190–191). Virtues are necessary in order to obtain such internal goods. MacIntyre defines a virtue as "*an acquired human quality the possession and exercise of which tends to enable us to achieve those goods internal to practices and the lack of which effectively prevents us from achieving any such goods*" (MacIntyre's italics, 1984: 191). Some virtues, according to MacIntyre, are necessary for any human practice, such as courage (the ability to take risks), justice, and honesty. Virtues also define the relationships between those who participate in a practice. For example, the virtue of beneficence (doing good), among others, defines the relationships between medical practitioners. Ideally, they develop habits which allow them to help their patients, and they work together toward that common end.

To identify the "goods internal" to a particular practice, one must identify the particular ends (*teloi*) of a practice without which the practice would not exist. This could involve polling participants in a practice, though this is not foolproof. A group of physicians employed by the Nazis in a concentration camp, for example, would not be the ideal group to ask about the goods internal to medicine. Alternatively, we could look to an individual universally acknowledged as an ideal participant in a particular practice (the equivalent of Aristotle's "person of practical wisdom," an ideal individual who is virtuous and can stand as an example to others) and examine his or her understanding of a practice's internal goods. However, to understand the richness of a practice as a whole, one should probably examine the practice itself, see what its practitioners do, their ideals, etc. (certainly looking to "ideal practitioners" will be part of the process), and then determine which goals are necessary and sufficient for the practice to be what it is.

Using medicine again as an example, even a cursory examination of the practice of medicine reveals that it involves people with special training in health care attempting to help sick or injured people. The fundamental internal goods of medicine must, therefore, involve helping a sick (or injured) person in need, and the fundamental standard of evaluation will be some form of return to health (or in the case of patients who cannot be returned to health, a lessening of their suffering). Thus, "helping a sick or injured person return to health" is a good internal to the practice of medicine. Certain virtues follow from this fundamental internal good, such as the courage to make difficult health-related decisions regarding a patient, justice, in the sense that patients should receive the same standard of care as much as possible (regardless of race, sex, religion, and socio-economic status), and truthfulness with the patient. The vulnerability of the patient and the greater knowledge and power of the physician make it easier – and more of a moral evil – for the physician to lie to a patient. The same patient vulnerability and power disparity between physician and patient make it an absolute moral evil for a health care practitioner to have sexual relations with a patient. Medicine, like all practices, is an inherently moral enterprise. A person claiming to practice medicine who violates the fundamental ends of medicine is engaged in deception – claiming to practice medicine when in fact he or she is no longer doing so. If someone denies that helping a sick or injured patient is the fundamental good of medicine (e.g., a hospital only concerned with the end profit without any concern for good patient care, other than as a means to profit), then something other than the practicing of medicine is going on. To deny the fundamental internal goods of a practice is, within the context of that practice, morally problematic, and is, in effect, a denial of the practice itself.

Business as a Practice

Is business a "practice" in MacIntyre's sense? Robert Solomon argues that it is. Disagreeing with the idea that the primary aim of business is making money, Solomon starts with the etymology of the word "business," which refers to "*activity*, being *occupied*, making oneself busy rather than making money as such.

Making or taking money is secondary, the result or reward of activity" (Solomon, 1993: 118). But more is needed:

> business is a quintessential *social* activity. It involves trading partners and consumers, at the very least, and it presupposes a network of implied and implicit understandings and agreements, a shared set of rituals (how to bargain, how to pay), more than a modicum of mutual trust and some underlying system of evaluation, only the details of which are settled in actual bargaining and negotiation. (Solomon, 1993: 118–119)

But the reality of business as social is still not enough to understand it as a practice. Solomon holds that, in addition, business "has goals and rules and boundaries and a purpose." He carefully distinguishes "purposes" and "goals." The ultimate goal of playing chess, for example, is to win the game by checkmating the opponent's king (unless the opponent resigns first, which is just as good). That goal is internal to the practice of chess, and it is that "internality" to a practice that distinguishes a "goal" from a "purpose." The purposes (reasons) for playing chess could be many things, ranging from enjoying a game that makes one think to just passing the time when one is bored. Solomon's "goals internal" to a practice are roughly equivalent to MacIntyre's "goods internal" to a practice. One point Solomon wishes to make clear is that profit is only one internal good of business, and not the most important one, and that it is certainly not the purpose of business: "It can and has been argued that profit making is not even a goal of business, but rather a condition of 'staying in the game,' a necessity and not an aspiration" (Solomon, 1993: 120–121). Solomon believes that the "goals internal to the practice [of business] might in general be summarized as 'doing well,' but 'doing well' is by no means limited to making profits" (Solomon, 1993: 121). For Solomon, purposes are more fundamental than goals for any practice. He holds that the purpose of business is "to provide for the prosperity of the entire society," "to provide the 'things that make ordinary life easier'" (Solomon, 1993: 122–123).

Those of us who participate in any practice, including business, are not isolated individuals pursuing independent ends, but are part of a human community "in which we learn to identify ourselves in terms of our positions and our roles, in conjunction with and in comparison and contrast with others. Our roles allow us to make certain choices but not others, allow and encourage certain agreements and not others" (Solomon, 1993: 79). One cannot just behave in any way he or she pleases in a particular role, whether that role be that of an administrative assistant or a CEO – even if he or she has the authority to do so. Not everything legally authorized is morally permissible.

Any practice, whether it be medicine, law, or business, is an essentially moral enterprise. As such, virtues are essential to the practice of business. Business is a type of community, or society, and it is "[t]he concept of the virtues [that] provides the conceptual linkage between the individual and his or her society. A virtue is a pervasive trait of character that allows one to 'fit into' a particular society and to excel in it" (Solomon, 1993: 107). Some virtues, such as honesty and courage, are necessary across human communities, but others are particular to specific practices. How virtues work within a practice is a contextual question, one which applies to all virtues, even the more "general" ones such as integrity (Solomon, 1993: 108–109). For example, in the context of a corporation, an

> emphasis on integrity and community [carries with it] not only the fulfillment of obligations to stockholders (not all of them "fiduciary") but the production of quality and the earning of pride in one's products, providing good jobs and well-deserved rewards for employees, and the enrichment of a whole community and not just a select group of (possibly short-term) contracted "owners." (Solomon, 1993: 109)

Solomon lists a number of virtues he believes are essential to the practice of business. These include the "basic business virtues" of honesty, fairness, trust, and toughness as well as virtues more specific to the "corporate self," such as friendliness, honor, loyalty, and shame. Other virtues, such as caring and compassion, are also essential (Solomon, 1993: chapters 19–21). But the "ultimate virtue of corporate life," according to Solomon, is justice (Solomon, 1993: 231). Since it is the virtue of justice that most clearly impacts the issue of executive compensation, I shall focus on Solomon's discussion in detail.

Why does Solomon believe that justice is so essential to corporate life? He argues persuasively that it is "not only a virtue," but also "is an utter necessity" (Solomon, 1993: 231). Without justice, the corporate community would fall apart:

> Justice, as "fairness," holds the institution together. As fairness, it is the fact *and perception* (italics mine, M.P.) that all members of the organization and everyone connected with it are "getting their due." In particular, this means that people get recognized for what they do and are properly rewarded with commendations, bonuses, and promotions, that people are hired into positions they deserve and given duties commensurate with their abilities and salary, that they are treated in times of crisis no differently from their peers and, of course, that they are paid and paid on time. (Solomon, 1993: 231)

Since a person finds much of his or her identity in the corporation, this strong bond between employee and corporation cannot be cemented by "affection" alone nor by "contractual arrangement." The "expectations and demands" involved are simply too complex. The employee must also have a sense that he or she "is being treated fairly" (Solomon, 1993: 231). If this does not occur, it leads to two vices which can be deadly to any corporation: envy and resentment (Solomon, 1993: chapter 23). As Solomon puts it, "Nothing fosters resentment faster than the perception that we are being paid less or given less recognition for our accomplishments than someone else, and that someone else is getting the rewards that we ourselves deserve" (Solomon, 1993: 232). He states that "the first rule of justice in business ethics must be 'equal work, equal pay.'" This is related to the ancient idea of justice as desert, the notion that justice involves people getting what they deserve. Another aspect of justice, which will also come into play in my discussion of executive compensation, is the idea that justice does not mean "might makes right." Might can be used for good or ill, for justice or injustice, but might does not itself constitute justice or injustice. A CEO who is ruthless with his or her employees, firing them for trivial reasons, may have the authority to be ruthless, but that does not mean that such ruthless actions are just.

Executive Compensation and Virtue

The issue of whether executive compensation is unjust in particular cases is not one that is subject to an algorithm. The issue of how much any employee should be paid, no matter what the position, is a difficult question to answer. What is fair pay for a maintenance worker? For a teacher? For a middle manager? For a CEO? These questions do not have exact answers. There are some general principles which might be applied; for example, usually, the higher the level of responsibility, the higher the level of pay. Thus, a physician is paid more than a nurse who is paid more than a technician. In business, managers are paid more than factory workers and the farther one travels up the executive scale, the higher the pay and benefits. What is considered to be "fair pay" is, at least in part, a matter of consensus within a particular practice, and even that may vary from location to location. This may itself be deceiving; higher salaries in California, for example, reflect, in part, the high cost of living there. Sometimes society, working through particular institutions, sets salaries; the US Congress, for example, sets the annual salary of the President and Vice-President of the United States. But this does not imply that the salaries of these officials is just; it might be argued that they are too low, much lower than even non-CEO executives in most corporations. Societal tolerance for high pay, such as society's tolerating multimillion-dollar contracts for professional athletes, does not necessarily imply that their level of compensation is not excessive. Pay may be considered unjust when there are serious inequities between workers on grounds irrelevant to skills or job performance. It is generally agreed to be unfair when a woman, who does the same job as a man, is paid much less than her male counterpart. It is similarly agreed to be unfair when a small business owner, who pays most of his employees minimum wage, and has a habit of laying off workers at the first sign of economic trouble, rakes in a six-digit income every year. He may have the legal authority to treat his employees in this way, but that does not make his behavior just. I argue that he lacks the virtue of justice and is violating the common good of the community – his business – and thus violates the very nature of business itself. If business is a community of persons oriented toward the end of bettering society economically, then a business owner taking a high salary at the expense of his workers is defrauding them, and this is fundamentally unjust. Cicero, like most ancient Greek and Latin writers, accepts a virtue-theory of ethics (though he differs from Aristotle on some points, being more eclectic, though tending to prefer Stoic doctrines). He was skeptical of any form of profit-oriented business, but he still has some useful things to say on the issue of taking what is not one's due.

> for a man to take something from a neighbour and to profit by his neighbour's loss is . . . contrary to Nature. For, in the first place, injustice is fatal to social life and fellowship between man and man. For, if we are so disposed that each, to gain some personal profit, will defraud or injure his neighbour, then those bonds of human society, which are most in accord with Nature's laws, must of necessity be broken. (Cicero, 1913: III.4.22)

If we replace "contrary to Nature" with "contrary to the goods (or goals) internal to business," then we have a better idea of why this business owner's actions are so flawed. By harming those employees who are members of his own community, he is violating the justice and trust necessary for any human community to work, including business. Practically speaking, workers will not be loyal to someone they perceive (rightly, in this case) as being unfair. At some level, trust and loyalty are needed for a company to prosper. Without these, this company will be left with a group of resentful, unhappy employees.

Even if the owner's employees (perhaps due to past poor economic circumstances) are "satisfied" with the minimum wage, this "satisfaction" does not make the owner's actions any less just, for he could afford to pay his employees more. The owner is taking advantage of his workers. Cicero goes on to say, "if the individual appropriates to selfish ends what should be devoted to the common good, all human fellowship will be destroyed" (Cicero, 1913: III.4.28). And such fellow-ship is not an option for business; it is a very part of the nature of business. Injustice destroys community, and thus destroys business, which is a form of community.

The same considerations can be applied to the pay of top corporate executives. When they are paid hundreds of times the salary of their average worker, when they receive not only multimillion-dollar salaries but also stock options, houses, free security, fine automobiles, and generous retirement packages, this comes across, at least, as unjust compensation. The sense of injustice deepens with high CEO compensation at the same time that shareholder earnings are dropping (in one case of a company with a highly paid CEO, shareholder returns dropped 91 percent) (*Business Week Online*, 2004). Even worse is the situation in which a "company gives bonuses to its top executives as employees and managers are being let go" (Solomon, 1993: 245). One CEO and chairman of the board made "$8.9 million in 2003, the same year that his company lost $463 million and he slashed the work force by 20 percent, or 6,000 workers" (The Associated Press, 2004). The envy and resentment resulting from such a sense of inequity and injustice will poison a corporation, will not inspire loyalty, and will encourage able employees to move around from company to company. What results from the injustice of excessive executive compensation is a loss of humanity within the corporation.

In 2003, "[m]any boards . . . began making pay more dependent on tough goals, limiting massive payouts," such as "shifting pay from options to restricted stock and replacing traditional options with those that pay off only after a big rise in stock prices" (Lavelle et al., 2004). Despite such limitations, *Business Week* notes that one should "[n]ever underestimate the ability of CEOs to find fresh sources of compensation" in the form of expensive perks (Lavelle et al., 2004). Peter Hodgson describes the motivation for such perks "as a case of keeping up with the Joneses. 'There's a 'he's getting it, so why shouldn't I?' aspect to it . . . It's a badge of merit'" (Lavelle et al., 2004). Instead of comparing their compensation packages to the other employees of their companies, CEOs are comparing them to other CEOs, hardly an adequate standard for just compensation, since the issue of inequity most often arises *within* a particular corporation.

Even if a company *has* done well in shareholder earnings, such profitability does not imply that the massive compensation packages for CEOs and other top executives are just. But first, to deal with what is a pseudo-problem with huge executive compensation packages: at least in the case of mega-corporations, it is probably not true that large-scale compensation for the CEO and top executives makes a significant impact on the overall finances of such corporations. Since a million dollars is often a "drop in the bucket" for a multibillion-dollar corporation, it is not necessarily the case that "giving to the CEO" is "taking from the rest of the employees." The situation is not zero-sum. That being said, there remain real problems with excessive executive pay. First, the success of the company is a team effort, and not merely the result of the actions of the CEO. It is true that the CEO has a greater measure of overall responsibility for the corporation, but corporations are too large and unwieldy to be governed by just one individual. It takes a large number of individuals, from the CEO to other senior executives to managers and supervisors to the workers at the bottom of the corporate ladder to make a corporation work. Instead of the CEO (and perhaps a few other top executives) receiving massive compensation packages, increased corporate profits could be spread to the other employees in the form of pay raises and/or other benefits, with profit left to spare to keep shareholders happy. More than shareholders are involved in a corporation in any case; the employees are obviously "stakeholders." The fact that their sense of identity is often closely tied to the company for which they work creates a greater responsibility for management to see that they are treated in a just and fair manner, including issues of pay. Even if stockholders do well, the employees may feel unjustly treated, asking why only the stockholders and the top executives should reap the benefits of increased profits.

Second, even if from some abstract point of view, one could argue that it is fair to compensate executives with huge packages if the stockholders do well, in the concrete context of the actual corporation, it may not be fair. Business is a practice; as such, it is an activity necessarily involving community. It involves real people with real lives and real feelings. If the employees of a corporation feel that they are being treated unjustly due to the difference between their own pay and the pay of top executives, this is *prima facie* evidence for the claim that they *are* being treated unjustly.[1] It is common, as Solomon points out, to ignore the role of feelings in business (and in business ethics), except for "the impoverished idea of *Homo economicus* who has no attachments or affections other than crude self-interest and the ability to calculate how to satisfy that interest vis-à-vis other

---

[1] This claim must be appropriately qualified, as use of *prima facie* to characterize the evidence indicates. I am not saying that when employees feel that the compensation package of a CEO is unjust, that these feelings are a sufficient condition for such compensation being unjust. Rather, such negative feelings among a vast majority of employees should be taken into account as genuine evidence that the compensation of a CEO may be unjust. Other, more "objective" factors, such as the ratio of CEO compensation to that of the typical employee, must come into play as well.

people" (Solomon, 1993: 220). Individuals have feelings of what is fair and not fair, and these feelings should not be ignored in the context of the community of the corporation. Although feelings can be wrongheaded, when a significant number of employees of a company believe that injustice is taking place, their feelings should be taken seriously. It is not necessarily greed that motivates employees to be upset about executive pay; it is the real sense that it is wrong for a CEO to make 300 times more than the average employee.[2] They may also have the sense, summarized in the oft-quoted saying, "Nobody needs that kind of money! What's he going to do with it?!" A more modest pay and benefit package for the CEO (and perhaps for other senior executives) can do much to alleviate this sense of injustice, and a virtuous CEO, one who has the virtue of justice, will act accordingly.

St Ambrose, one of the early Christian "Church Fathers" and Bishop of Milan in Italy, has an extensive discussion of the proper virtues of the clergy. Ambrose was no friend of business, since he agreed with Cicero and accepted the widely held view that profit was a form of theft; however, much of what he says can be applied to executives considering their compensation packages. He states:

> The rule of economy and the authority of self-restraint befits all, and most of all him who stands highest in honour; so that no love for his treasures should seize upon such a man, and that he who rules over free men may never become a slave to money. It is more seemly in soul that he should be superior to treasures, and in willing service be subject to his friends. (St. Ambrose, 1989: II.14.87)

There is a role for self-restraint among CEOs and other top executives. Even if some of them are not "slaves to money" in the sense of wanting it for its own sake, there remains the temptation (also found among professional athletes when they are negotiating their salaries) to "make as much money (or more money) that other CEOs." This is not to say that CEOs should not be rewarded with extra pay or bonuses when the company does well; it is to say that such benefits should be moderate and not excessive. According to David Callahan, moderation in CEO pay was the trend in US corporations from the 1940s to the 1960s. During that time, "top executives understood that they would not be granted salaries that

---

[2] The ratio of CEO compensation to that of the typical employee of a corporation is only one factor that should be considered regarding just CEO compensation. The financial condition of the company should be considered, as well as CEO performance. Also, in smaller corporations, a smaller ratio of CEO compensation to the typical employee's pay may be unjust. So much depends on the circumstances of the individual corporation.

too greedily dwarfed those of average workers" (Callahan, 2004: 94). CEO pay in 1965 was "an average 50 times more than the typical worker," as opposed to "nearly 300 times" today (Callahan, 2004: 94). And when pay was more modest, CEOs often lived a lifestyle that could be compared to that of other workers, preferring to live in relatively modest homes and drive moderately priced cars. There was a greater sense of propriety, Callahan believes, among CEOs at that time than today (Callahan, 2004: 94–95). By practicing self-restraint, these CEOs were contributing to a more just corporation.

Another temptation discussed by St Ambrose is the tendency to value individuals only on the basis of the amount of money that they make. As he puts it, "man's habits have so long applied themselves to this admiration of money that no one is thought worthy of honour unless he is rich" (St. Ambrose, 1989: II. 26.129.). It may be this sense of honor for greater compensation that is part of the motivation for high executive pay. But executives can be compensated well without such compensation becoming excessive; what is "excessive" will vary from corporation to corporation, depending on the attitude of the other employees and the culture of that particular corporation. The value of what the CEO has accomplished for the corporation will not be lost if he or she does not get an extra $10 million a year.

Probably the most serious difficulty with high CEO compensation is the focus on the individual over the good of the corporation as a whole. This is *not* the same as the claim that paying the CEO more takes money from others. The problem is that excessive CEO pay may be good for the CEO (though with the amount of money and perks involved, one can legitimately question how much of a good more money could be), but it is not for the good for the community of the corporation as a whole. A morally virtuous leader in business will consider the general good when considering his or her compensation, even putting it over his or her own desires. As St Ambrose states, "all must consider and hold that the advantage of the individual is the same as that of all, and that nothing can be considered advantageous except what is for the general good. For how can one be benefited alone?" (St. Ambrose, 1989: III.4.25). Now the CEO may have a great deal of "pull" with the board of directors, especially if the company is doing well, and may realize he or she will get most of the pay and benefits, which he or she requests. But "might does not make right," and neither the desire of the CEO for a high level of compensation nor the desire of the board of directors to grant such compensation makes that right. The board of directors and the CEO should keep the good of the entire corporation, including the lowest-paid employee, in mind. The CEO is not some isolated individual seeking his or her own ends independently of other members of the corporate community; he or she is part of the whole. The CEO's role is defined by the corporation. The corporation has an overall purpose to benefit society by providing quality goods and/or services, and there are also "goals internal" to any corporation. One of these internal goals is to treat employees well, to treat them as human beings, not as mere cogs in a machine, to pay them fair wages and salaries, to treat all of them with justice. It is the nature of goals/goods internal to any practice that if someone violates them, that individual has placed him or herself outside of that practice. For example, if a physician refuses to treat a patient he does not like personally, that physician is violating the fundamental end of medicine to help a sick or injured person in need. He has placed himself outside the practice of medicine, even though he may still keep the trappings of a physician. Or if a business executive discriminates against someone due to her race, that executive is violating the virtue most fundamental to the practice of business, justice, without which a business could not exist as a practice. In a sense, such an executive is no longer "doing business" but something else, since the virtue of justice is fundamental to the "goals internal" to business. Thus, a CEO who takes a huge compensation package, thinking only of his or her own benefit and "reputation," is being unjust and is practicing something other than "business."

What all this means for practical policy will depend on the particular corporation. Each corporation has its own unique history, ethic, and group of employees. Thus, to set a particular salary limit for CEOs and other top executives across the board for all corporations would ignore the focus on particularity that is characteristic of the virtue approach to ethics. Nevertheless, CEOs can set an example of virtue by focusing on the good of the corporation as a whole. If a CEO sees that a particular compensation package will lead to a huge gap between his or her own salary and the corporation's average employee's salary, a CEO with the virtue of justice would have that package reduced. If the company is in trouble and there is a need for layoffs, this increases the responsibility of all senior management, especially the CEO, not to accept increases in compensation and to consider reductions in compensation. Although such a legalistic approach is not ideal, boards of directors may set limitations on executive compensation – but some executives will be able to find creative ways to circumvent such limitations. Cases in which a CEO receives major benefits for company success in increasing shareholder earnings may reduce employees' sense of inequity, since such compensation is merit-based. However, huge gaps between executive and average employee pay fuel a sense of inequity, and a wise and just CEO would consider increase of pay and benefits for the other employees of the corporation.

The virtue approach to CEO pay has advantages over alternative approaches, such as utilitarian or deontological approaches. It is not overly formalistic like the deontological approach and is also more flexible due to its focus on particular situations in particular corporations: "How much should *this* CEO in *this* corporation be paid *in these circumstances*?" Unlike the utilitarian approach, the virtue approach focuses on more than consequences (though it does not deny their role in ethics) and emphasizes the concrete nature of business life, as well as the characters of those who participate in the practice of business. In the debate over CEO compensation, virtue ethics goes beyond the bottom line of compensation versus stockholder earnings to focus on how a particular corporation with its particular ethic and employees views justice when it comes to executive pay. Although the virtue approach does not offer specific algorithms for executive compensation, it welcomes the richness of corporate life in all its ambiguity. It recognizes that the corporation is a community of persons working toward a common end that requires specific internal goals and virtuous persons in order to survive. (If anyone thinks that the lack of virtue in executives does not have practical consequences, the Enron case is a good counterexample). If CEOs are virtuous, putting the good of the many over their own individual wants, then the public resentment over excessive CEO compensation (and most likely, the excessive compensation of other executives) would be greatly mitigated.

ACKNOWLEDGMENTS

I am grateful to my colleague at Methodist College, Dr Michael Colonese, for proofreading the paper and for his suggestions for improvement. I am also grateful to all those who have made comments and criticisms of this paper at the 2004 Japha Symposium.

REFERENCES

Business Week Online. 2004. "Pay for Performance: CEOs at Both Ends of the Scale," April 19, at http://www.businessweek.com/magazine/content/04_16/b3879015.htm, accessed May 29, 2004.

Callahan, David. 2004. *The Cheating Culture: Why More Americans are Doing Wrong to Get Ahead.* Orlando: Harcourt, Inc., p. 94

Cicero, Marcus Tullius. 1913. *De Officiis,* [trans. Walter Miller, Loeb Classical Library], Cambridge, MA: Harvard University Press.

Lavelle, Louis, Hempel, Jessi, and Brady, Diane. 2004. Executive pay. *Business Week Online,* April 19, available at http://www.businessweek.com/print/magazine/content/04_16/b3879010.htm?mz, accessed May 29, 2004.

MacIntyre, Alasdair. 1984. *After Virtue: A Study in Moral Theory,* 2nd edn. Notre Dame, IN: University of Notre Dame Press.

Solomon, Robert C. 1993. *Ethics and Excellence: Cooperation and Integrity in Business.* New York and Oxford: Oxford University Press, p. 118

St Ambrose, 1989. Duties of the clergy [trans. H. de Romestin, E. de Romestin, and H. T. F. Duckworth]. In Philip Shaff and Henry Wace, eds., *A Select Library of Nicene and Post-Nicene Fathers of the Christian Church,* 2nd series, vol. X, *St. Ambrose: Selected Works and Letters,* reprint edn. Edinburgh: T&T Clark; Grand Rapids, MI: William B. Eerdmans Publishing Company.

Sternberg, Elaine. 2000. Just Business: Business Ethics in Action, 2nd edn. Oxford: Oxford University Press, p. 216.

The Associated Press. 2004. "Some Say Executive Salaries Excessive," *The Indianapolis Star,* April 25, at http://www.indystar.com/articles/4/141210-1304-P.html, accessed May 24, 2004.

7

Chihuahuas in the Gardens of Corporate Capitalism

Lyla D. Hamilton
Center for Business and Society, Leeds School of Business, University of
Colorado, Boulder, CO

Introduction

You know that concern about executive compensation has reached a boiling point
when *Corporate Board Member Magazine* publishes – without even a whisper of a
challenge – an article that claims: "Our system [of compensation] is fundamentally
flawed ethically, legally and economically." (Van Clieaf, 2004)

The authors in this section have considered the ethics of executive compensation
as a question of justice. Potts, for example, holds that a CEO who possesses the
virtue of justice would prefer a compensation package that has an appropriate relationship to the compensation of the corporation's average employee. Harris and
Shaw explore the issue of executive compensation within the framework of major
theories of distributive justice.

This chapter draws attention to another dimension of justice, the principle
of fidelity or promise keeping, and its implications for executive compensation.
It also considers the purpose of business.

Promises, Promises

Imagine a rather ordinary promise between two people. One enjoys gardening
and each summer produces a bountiful crop of vegetables. A neighbor would
delight in having fresh home-grown vegetables but has no interest in gardening.
Upon discussion, the two reach a congenial arrangement: the person who enjoys
gardening will select appropriate plants and tend them; the other will pay the
costs of the plants and a portion of the gardener's water bill during the growing
season. They will share the harvest, with half going to the gardener, three-eighths
to the neighbor, and the remainder to a local food bank.

We ordinarily think that a promise made under certain conditions (e.g., it is voluntary) should be kept. Hence, if the neighbor fulfils his obligation – barring circumstances that would invalidate the promise – we believe the gardener is obligated to distribute the harvest as agreed. If he fails to do so, we think it proper to call him to account and to demand that he fulfill his obligation (Rawls, 1971: 342–350).

While corporations are more complex arrangements than this neighborly agreement, the principle is the same. In exchange for the use of investors' capital, corporate managers and executives promise to serve investors' interests. Board members also make a promise: they agree to make diligent and good-faith efforts to see to it that the organization does not fall prey to the problem of agency. In plain English, they accept the responsibility of doing their best to ensure that corporate managers and executives pursue the interests of the investors rather than their own.

What seems to have happened in recent cases of excessive executive compensation is that corporate board members have failed to fulfill this obligation. The Conference Board Commission on Public Trust and Private Enterprise bluntly says, "Boards of directors became lax in performing their historical duty to monitor compensation" (Peterson & Snow, 2002: 6). Legendary investor Warren Buffett is characteristically more colorful in making the point. He complains: "The typical large company has a compensation committee. They do not look for Dobermans on that committee. They look for Chihuahuas that have been sedated" (Zweig, 2004).

Continuous benchmarking of executive compensation packages has led to continuous increases. As the Conference Board Commission (Peterson & Snow, 2002: 6) points out, however, not all company executives can be in the top quartile of pay scales. Compensation committees have hesitated to address the obvious implications of this fact. They have endorsed pay packages that lack any plausible grounding in executive performance and contribution.

Those of us who struggle to achieve fairness in grading students, face a similar challenge in what's been called the "Lake Woebegone Effect," named for the mythical place where "all the children are above average."

If breach of the board's fiduciary responsibility to investors is a core issue in the problem of excessive executive compensation, then enforcement of that responsibility seems an appropriate recourse. As it happens, the promise that board members make has legal as well as moral weight; corporate board members have legal obligations as fiduciaries.

Accordingly, shareholders, prosecutors, and the courts have sought recourse by demanding that board members live up to these obligations. Shareholders, for example, have advanced proxy proposals regarding executive compensation.

In Germany, Josef Ackermann, head of Deutsche Bank, was charged with "breach of trust" allegedly committed while he was on the board and compensation committee of Mannesmann during a takeover that yielded $53 million as bonus to a group of Mannesmann executives (*Economist*, 2004). While Ackermann and five other former directors, employees, and managers were cleared of criminal charges in 2004, prosecutors have asked for a retrial (Bloomberg, 2004).

In litigation regarding the compensation package granted Walt Disney Company President Michael Ovitz, the Delaware Court of Chancery, which is influential because many large companies are incorporated in Delaware, held that "[w]here a director consciously ignores his or her duties to the corporation, thereby causing economic injury to its shareholders, the director's actions are either 'not in good faith' or 'involve intentional misconduct.'" Both findings strip from the director any protection provided by Directors and Officers insurance and makes him or her personally liable for damages to shareholders (*Corporate Board Member Magazine*, 2004b).

Litigation against board members is not the only form of recourse available in matters of excessive executive compensation. As we might demand possession of the vegetables the recalcitrant gardener has unjustly retained, we might demand that the overpaid executive relinquish "ill-gotten gains." In other words, another remedy for the injustice of excessive executive pay is disgorgement, a solution being sought in the case of Richard Grasso, former chairman of the New York Stock Exchange. It has already been accepted in a suit regarding the compensation paid to Cendant's CEO. The negotiated settlement required the executive to give up a substantial portion of his pay package (*Corporate Board Member Magazine*, 2004).

The fact that shareholders, prosecutors, and courts can call board members and executives to account does not mean that the situation regarding executive compensation is rosy – or even barely satisfactory from the standpoint of justice. My point is simply that we can find a plausible explanation of the injustice of excessive executive compensation – and some possible responses to that injustice – through the principle of fidelity or promise keeping.

Let me emphasize that I do not believe that principles of distributive justice are irrelevant to executive compensation. Rather, I believe that they enter the issue in a framework defined by the principle of fidelity and the obligation of each person, regardless of role, to uphold justice. In the negotiations and deliberations of corporate boards (and especially compensation committees) and corporate executives, then, all parties need to consider not only what they're willing to agree to, but what is fair *within the context of their responsibilities to investors and their duties to uphold justice* (Rawls, 1971: 114–116).

From this, it should be clear that I do not endorse the view Professor Shaw attributes to Robert Nozick: that a level of executive compensation is just if and only if all parties freely agree to it. On the contrary, I'm suggesting that corporate board members are not at liberty to make just any agreement on matters that lie within the scope of their responsibilities as board members: they are bound by their obligation to protect investors' interests as well as by principles of justice. While they might in fact accept the terms of a compensation package incompatible with that obligation and those principles, to do so would be unjust.

Some Reflections on the Purpose of Business

Having considered how the principle of promise keeping help us understand the injustice of excessive executive compensation, I want to turn to the purpose of business, a theme that runs through Professor Potts' essay in particular. As he notes, philosopher Robert Solomon declared some years ago that the purpose of business is "to provide for the prosperity of the entire society". A decade before that, Harvard Business School Professor Theodore Levitt roundly rejected the view – widely held then and now – that the purpose of business is to generate profits. He found that claim as vacuous as saying the purpose of life is to eat. "Eating," Levitt says, "is a requisite, not a purpose of life. Without eating, life stops." Similarly, he says, "Profits are a requisite of business. Without profits, business stops." (Levitt, 1983: 6) What then, does Levitt think is the purpose of business? He believes it is to create and keep a customer (Levitt, 1983: 5).

This idea may seem bizarre. It *is* bizarre if you see the world from the perspective of corporate capitalism. Consumer packaged goods companies like Kraft and Procter & Gamble, for example, typically define customers based on demographic characteristics. They may seek to sell a particular brand to

- Married Hispanic women aged 25–35
- Males aged 11–21 who own 9 or more video games
- Homeowners with gross incomes exceeding $1 million per year

How can companies create more customers – more people in any of those demographic groups? They cannot, of course.

They therefore look for ways to sell more and different products to people: yet another way to package soap, pudding, and toothpaste; or different container sizes for sugar water. They even, according to a recent *Wall Street Journal* article, produce electrically powered air fresheners that deliver a different scent every 30 minutes lest our olfactory nerves become bored. Companies euphemistically term this satisfying "unmet needs" (Ball et al., 2004). This disingenuousness – to describe it politely – can make it hard to take capitalism and capitalists seriously.

I nevertheless believe we can regard business as a morally serious endeavor, though I might not join theologian and sociologist Michael Novak in characterizing it as a "calling" or "vocation" (Novak, 1996: 13). If we conceive of business as one of the several social means of identifying and addressing human needs, we have the beginnings of a moral rationale for the institution: it is about needs and not (just) greed or acquisitiveness.

Through creative genius – whether embodied in an individual or a group – we no longer launder our clothes by beating them on rocks in a river. Nor do we rub them and a tablet of homemade lye soap against a metal washboard. Nor do we force garments through a hand-powered wringer. We can entrust them to an energy- and water-efficient machine that uses environmentally friendly cleaning agents.

If business is a means of identifying and addressing human needs, its top achievers are those who create solutions to problems – sometimes problems we did not know we had or which we had no affordable way to solve. The heroes are not those who can manipulate the numbers or fool people into purchasing junk.

Some who choose careers in business seek to acquire. Others, however, seek to create. A possible example is Jim Sinegal, president and CEO of Costco Inc., who says that of all of the company's accomplishments, what he is proudest of is the creation of an employee base of 102,000 employees who are paid well, get full benefits, and "who see Costco as a career, not a job" (Hightower, 2004).

Lest you think this an empty platitude, please note that Costco's employees are among the best paid in the retail industry. Sinegal opposes excessive executive compensation and he practices what he preaches (Zimmerman, 2004). While he probably is not representative of the way corporate executives behave, I do not think he is alone in exhibiting restraint – and perhaps even virtue – regarding compensation.

Once we consider the possibility that business is a creative and morally worthy undertaking, I think we can begin to make sense of the idea of creating a customer. Here I draw on a realm far from academe – the world of small, entrepreneurial, technology-focused ventures.

In the early 1970s, traditional quantitative market analysis would have found no demand for computers designed for use in the home. "The numbers" and "hard facts" rarely endorse a quantum leap. Ken Olson, then President of the now-defunct Digital Equipment Corporation, famously announced that he could not imagine a reason that anyone would want a computer at home.

Steve Jobs and Steve Wozniak could. They saw how people could use the technology to solve problems that seemed intractable (like managing their finances without spending hours with a calculator) or merely annoying (like keeping track of the people to whom they send holiday greetings). *This* is the sense in which Apple Computer created the customer for the personal computer; the company recognized a need and a way to meet it.

Corporate capitalism – a world of huge organizations with billions of dollars in assets – tempts us to regard distributive justice as the fundamental issue in executive compensation. After all, a lot of wealth exists; a lot of money is changing hands. It seems outrageous that some can comfortably spend thousands of dollars on shower curtains and antique umbrella stands while others struggle to subsist on contaminated water and moldy grain. I agree. Executive looters share responsibility with board members whose inattentiveness would offend any self-respecting Chihuahua. Both have failed to adhere to principles of fairness and fidelity.

The entrepreneurial form of capitalism reminds us, however, that jobs, benefits, and wealth – like fresh vegetables from the neighbor's garden – do not predate the investment of human, social, and financial capital. They are not always there to be distributed; sometimes they must be created. Honoring the promises made to investors is critical to sustaining that creative process.

REFERENCES

Ball, D., Ellison, S., and Adamy, J. 2004. Just what you need! *The Wall Street Journal*, October 28, B1, B8.

Bloomberg. 2004. German prosecutor seeks retrial in Mannesmann case. Retrieved October 28, 2004 from: http://quote.bloomberg.com/apps/news?pid=10000100&sid=ahm9cH7y XYq0&refer=germany.

Corporate Board Member Magazine. 2004. The new compensation committee responsibilities. Retrieved October 27, 2004 from: http://www.boardmember.com/network/index.pl?section=1038&article_id12028&show=article.

Economist. 2004. Fat cats feeding. Retrieved October 23, 2004 from: http://www.economist.com/business/globalexecutive/toolkit/printerFriendly.cfm?story_id=2153781.

Hightower, J. 2004. Costco sees value in higher pay. *Los Angeles Times*, February 15. Retrieved April 8, 2004 from http://www.jimhightower.com.

Levitt, T. 1983. *The Marketing Imagination*. New York: The Free Press.

Novak, M. 1996. *Business as a Calling*. New York: The Free Press.

Peterson, P. and Snow, J. 2002. *The Conference Board Commission on Public Trust and Private Enterprise, Findings, and Recommendations – Part 1: Executive Compensation.* New York: The Conference Board.

Rawls, J. 1971. *A Theory of Justice.* Cambridge, MA: Harvard University Press.

Van Clieaf, M. 2004. Statistics show need for executive compensation overhaul. *Corporate Board Member Magazine*, May 29. Retrieved October 27, 2004 from: http://www.boardmember.com/network/index.pl?section=1038&article_id=11903&show=article.

Zimmerman, A. 2004. Costco's dilemma: be kind to its workers, or Wall Street? *The Wall Street Journal*, March 26, B1, B3.

Zweig, J. 2004. What Warren Buffett wants you to know. *CNNMoney*, May 3. Retrieved October 23, 2004 from: http://money.cnn.com.

PART III

Broadening the Perspective

The question of executive compensation has attracted much attention and thought. Perhaps not surprisingly, such a broad social issue generates rather far-reaching considerations that may not at first be apparent. The chapters in this part point toward some potential solutions and some social ramifications of executive compensation that might not be apparent at first. In doing so, each chapter echoes some themes introduced by others in this volume.

Carmen M. Alston locates the central issue of executive compensation in the area of fiduciary responsibility in her chapter, "The Obligation of Corporate Boards to Set and Monitor Compensation." As the title implies, and consonant with Hamilton's approach that concluded the last part of this volume, Alston believes that executive compensation is excessive and that such pay could be constrained by boards of directors that fulfilled their responsibilities more fully. In examining this issue, Alston considers the responsibilities and powers of boards and makes specific suggestions for reform that will lead to a resolution of the problem of executive compensation.

Issues of executive compensation do not arise only in corporations governed by boards of directors. James Stacey Taylor finds similar issues in another sphere in his chapter, "Executive Pay in Public Academia: A Nonjustice-Based Argument for the Reallocation of Compensation." Taylor believes that state-sponsored academic institutions have missions that are quite different from corporations. As such, the grounds on which one might justify large differences in pay across different groups of workers in a public university diverge from those that might apply to corporations. Taylor argues that compensation within a public university is essentially a zero-sum game in contrast to a corporation and that one of the key purposes of a university is to foster personal autonomy. From this perspective, Taylor goes on to maintain that these considerations require restricting the pay of administrators of public universities on grounds that are quite different from those that might apply to the executives of a corporation.

Jeffrey Moriarty returns to the issues of justice in his chapter, "How to (Try to) Justify CEO Pay." Moriarty considers executive compensation under three views of what would constitute just compensation: the agreement view, the desert view, and the utility view. Even within the framework of each single view, Moriarty finds that executive compensation must be judged excessive. He then goes on to propose specific changes in corporate governance to alleviate the lack of justice that he finds.

To conclude the volume, Joseph DesJardins considers each of the three chapters in this part in turn in "Executive Compensation: Just Procedures and Outcomes." In doing so, though he highlights the fact that the issue of executive compensation remains unresolved, yet he points the way toward conceptual progress as he evaluates each chapter. For instance, DesJardins challenges Alston's view on the role of governmental regulation in the setting of executive compensation. Similarly, DesJardins calls into question Taylor's emphasis on the fostering of personal autonomy as a key goal of universities. Finally, DesJardins again turns to the issue of justice as he considers an analogy between the compensation of corporate executives and attorney contingent compensation fees in lawsuits. While acknowledging important differences, DesJardins is concerned enough to stress the importance of free agreement and the role of key individuals, whether corporate executives or effective trial attorneys, in creating the economic value at issue.

8

The Obligation of Corporate Boards to Set and Monitor Compensation

Carmen M. Alston
PhD Learner, Capella University, 13506 Wesley Oaks Drive, Houston, TX 77085

Introduction

One of the key fiduciary responsibilities of the corporate board is to set and monitor CEO compensation. However, over the past 20 years, average CEO compensation has increased to a level that many believe is excessive and that some deem unethical. Ultimately, it is the responsibility of the corporate board to structure a compensation package that provides the CEO with adequate incentives to act in the best short- and long-term interests of the firm. If recent events are any indication, however, the system of checks and balances in US business that expects the corporate board to determine CEO compensation that serves the shareholders' interests seems to have broken down (Anonymous, 2003). An examination of the underlying ethical issues that have led to the failure of boards to rein in CEO compensation is important in understanding how the situation has developed and in the steps that may be taken to correct it. This chapter will examine the role of the corporate board in setting and monitoring CEO compensation.

Background

Problem Statement

One of the key fiduciary responsibilities of the corporate board is to set and monitor CEO compensation. However, over the past 20 years, average CEO compensation has increased to a level that is believed excessive by many and unethical by some. During the 1980s, formulas used to calculate CEO compensation evolved from the traditional base salary plus a bonus that was tied to achievement of financial targets (Wilhelm, 1993). The new formulas included factors such as quality improvement, cash flow, and the buying and selling of firm assets in the compensation calculation (Wilhelm, 1993). As a result, according to Wilhelm, it became possible for CEOs to realize significant increases in pay even if their companies performed poorly overall.

By 1993, CEO pay had increased annually, surpassing increases in inflation and in average company profits, and about 60 percent of managers surveyed believed CEOs were paid too much (Wilhelm, 1993). The dramatic increases have sparked a great deal of research and debate on executive compensation, particularly around issues of fairness, equity, market efficiency, and leadership effectiveness (Carr & Valinezhad, 1994). The basic question explored by researchers is whether CEO pay is in fact excessive, or if it is an accurate reflection of the rewards a CEO has earned for his or her leadership and performance (Carr & Valinezhad, 1994).

Overwhelmingly, researchers have found either nonexistent or very weak links between the pay a CEO earns and the effectiveness of his or her leadership and performance (Carr & Valinezhad, 1994). Further, many have found evidence to suggest that the most popular formulas used to calculate CEO pay today actually serve as an incentive to the CEO to execute his or her duties in a manner that may be harmful to the firm's shareholders (Carr & Valinezhad, 1994). Carr and Valinezhad conclude that even a CEO who is essentially ethical may still rationally respond to financial incentives that conflict with the long-term effectiveness of the firm.

Ultimately, it is the responsibility of the corporate board to structure a compensation package that provides the CEO with adequate incentives to act in the best short- and long-term interests of the firm. If recent events are any indication, however, the system of checks and balances in the US business, which would have the corporate board determining CEO compensation that serves the shareholders' interests, seems to have broken down (Anonymous, 2003). An examination of the underlying ethical issues that have led to the failure of boards to rein in CEO compensation is important in understanding how the situation has developed and in the steps that may be taken to correct it.

Purpose of this Chapter

This chapter will examine the role of the corporate board in setting and monitoring CEO compensation, the ethical theories that have been used as justification for the design of CEO compensation packages, and the flaws in these theories that have led to excessive increases in CEO pay. Some of the reasons why corporate boards have been unwilling or unable to control CEO compensation will be discussed, and recommendations will be made for changes in corporate governance that will enable corporate boards to improve the effectiveness of their performance in this critical area of responsibility.

The Role of the Corporate Board in Setting and Monitoring CEO Compensation

Fiduciary Responsibility for CEO Compensation and Firm Performance

The corporate board is legally elected by the shareholders as the ultimate governing body of the corporation (George, 2002). According to George, the corporate board "is charged with preserving the company and building it for the long term" (p. 794). Arguably, the corporate board's primary duty is to protect shareholder interests by ensuring that the CEO fulfills his or her responsibilities to the firm to the full extent possible (Buchholtz et al., 1998). One of the most potent control mechanisms that the corporate board possesses, second only to their ability to hire and terminate the CEO, is the ability to design an incentive package that rewards the CEO for performance that serves the long-term interests of the shareholders (Buchholtz et al., 1998).

According to Buchholtz et al. (1998), "Governance theorists and shareholders alike contend that boards of directors best serve shareholder interests by establishing strong connections between CEO pay and firm performance" (p. 6). This assertion persists, despite the lack of evidence that the most popular formulas for calculating CEO compensation result in a meaningful link between CEO compensation and the firm's performance (Carr & Valinezhad, 1994). CEO compensation is also "related to the magnitude of the responsibility, risk, and effort shouldered by the CEO as a function of firm's scale, complexity and risk of the firm's operations" (Cordeiro & Veliyath, 2003).

Further, when determining the CEO's compensation, the corporate board should assess the CEO's leadership in terms of ethics and values (Anonymous, 2003). The beliefs and values that are exhibited throughout the firm will tend to be a reflection of those practiced by the senior leaders. The board must also model the ethics they expect the CEO and others to embody in the management of the firm (Anonymous, 2003).

Recent events would seem to suggest that many corporate boards are not acting as strong role models for ethical behavior. George (2002) concludes:

> In recent years many boards appear to have abandoned their legal and fiduciary responsibilities. They have become more responsive to the CEO and management than to the shareholders. In doing so, they abandoned their governance role and jumped on the bandwagon to get the company's stock price up. They stopped asking the hard questions about how the company was achieving its numbers, whether it was making adequate investments to build the company for the long-term, and whether its strategies were still valid and being effectively implemented. (p. 794)

Ethical Theories Underlying CEO Compensation

Agency Theory

The influence of agency theory may be found within many corporate governance and management control practices (Ekanayake, 2004). According to Ekanayake, "The premise of agency theory is that agents are self-interested, risk-averse, rational actors, who will always attempt to exert less effort (moral hazards) and project higher capabilities and skills than they actually have (adverse selections)" (p. 49). With this in mind, proper control mechanisms must be developed and enforced to prevent self-centered opportunistic managers from neglecting their responsibilities and violating the rights of shareholders (Carr & Valinezhad, 1994). The role of the control mechanisms is to curb the opportunistic behavior of managers by reducing the managers' incentives to behave in this manner (Ekanayake, 2004).

In utilizing agency theory as the basis for determining CEO compensation, the corporate board is attempting to solve two problems; the inability to monitor the CEO's behavior and the CEO's attitude toward risk (Ekanayake, 2004). Agency theory implies that it is very difficult or even impossible for the board to closely monitor the CEO's behavior; therefore, the focus will tend to be on the firm's outcomes (Ekanayake, 2004). Additionally, the agency theory recognizes that as the uncertainty and risk considerations increase for the CEO, the CEO's incentives to perform must also increase (Ekanayake, 2004).

Some agency theorists argue that salary by itself does not necessarily promote CEO performance that enhances shareholder value; however, pay-for-performance incentives do enable more equitable sharing of risks between the CEO and the shareholders (Cordeiro & Veliyath, 2003). By compensating the CEO with stock or granting the CEO the option to purchase stock at a favorable price, the corporate board is in effect making the CEO a shareholder in the firm (Bruhl, 2003). In theory, the CEO would then perform in the best interests of the shareholders because he or she is also now a shareholder.

The fundamental flaw in this theory is demonstrated in the implementation. Conflict generally arises when the corporate board is determining how tightly to link the CEO's compensation to performance. The shareholders would prefer a very tight link to provide maximum incentive to the CEO to perform in their interests; however, a tight link increases the financial risk to the CEO because there are many factors that are difficult to control that may adversely impact the firm's outcomes (Buchholtz et al., 1998).

If pay and performance are not strongly linked, on the other hand, the CEO may pursue projects at the expense of shareholder return because they may provide benefits to the CEO (Buchholtz et al., 1998). For example, increases in CEO compensation have been positively correlated to firm growth; therefore, the CEO may pursue growth that does not result in any meaningful benefit to the shareholders (Buchholtz et al., 1998).

Even if the corporate board does establish strong links between CEO pay and performance, it is a fallacy to assume that the CEO who has been rewarded with stock or stock options is the same as any other shareholder. Unlike the average shareholder, the CEO has access to inside information that would enable him or her to sell his or her stock at the optimal time to maximize his or her compensation (Bruhl, 2003). The CEO may also be motivated by the potential returns to take actions, or to manipulate or even falsify information to facilitate a short-term gain in the stock price at the long-term expense of the shareholders.

Stockholder Theory

Many of the pay for performance models utilized to design CEO compensation packages also reflect elements of stockholder theory. According to stockholder theory, the stockholders are the owners of the firm and are entitled to all the profits generated by the firm. The CEO is hired to serve as the agent of the stockholders and has a moral obligation to manage the firm in the best interests of the stockholders, which includes avoiding conflicts of interest in which it may appear that the CEO is benefiting at the expense of the stockholders (Beauchamp & Bowie, 2004).

Pay for performance compensation plans are designed to provide incentives for the CEO to initiate strategies that boost future stock performance, as indicated by factors such as accounting performance and stock market returns (Cordeiro & Veliyath, 2003). One of the most-often heard criticisms of pay for performance compensation models is that the firm's performance would not be possible without the contributions of most of the firm's employees, yet the CEO receives compensation for firm performance that may be several hundred times that received by the average employee (Wilhelm, 1993).

Defenders of current CEO pay for performance models would argue, however, that the CEO's contribution to the firm's success is in fact considerably more unique and valuable than that of the average employee, thus the extreme difference in salary is justified (Nichols & Subramaniam, 2001). The size of the recent pay increase is further justified by the increased challenges in the CEO's role due to factors such as rapidly changing technology, hypercompetitive markets, and global business operations (Nichols & Subramaniam, 2001).

In many organizations that utilize pay for performance models to determine the CEO's compensation, however, the amount of the CEO's pay has been found to be related more to the size of the firm, market share, or to sales volume, rather than to profits (Wilhelm, 1993). According to Wilhelm, "It is not surprising that CEO pay has been associated with company size, that is, the larger the company the bigger the paycheck. There is little correlation between how large a company is, measured by revenue, and how well it performs for the stockholders or in its markets" (p. 476). Gago and Rodgers (2003) have found that less than 5 percent of the average CEO's total pay is explained by financial information performance factors.

Stockholder theory as a basis for CEO compensation is further eroded when the compensation package includes stock or stock options. Stock options were initially viewed by the corporate board as an ideal long-term incentive for the CEO to work to increase the shareholder value because the CEO would generally have up to 10 years to exercise the options to purchase stock at today's price (Hardin et al., 1995). Stock options as compensation had the added advantage of being viewed as free by the corporate board and the CEO, because they had no cash impact and were not charged against the firm's profits (George, 2002).

Instead of motivating CEOs to focus on the long-term growth of the firm's stock price, however, many have instead chosen to take short-term actions that do not create real shareholder value, but do increase the price of the stock in the short-term so that the CEO may receive an optimal return when he or she exercises his or her options (Hardin et al., 1995). And in another breach of their fiduciary responsibility, corporate boards have frequently agreed to reprice the options so that the CEO may be rewarded even if the stock price has fallen since the options were originally granted (Hardin et al., 1995). The practice of repricing options due to a drop in stock price completely mitigates the value of stock options as a long-term incentive (Alam et al., 2000).

Social Comparison and Inequity Theories

Social inequity theory contends that inequity exists if one perceives that the ratio of his or her output to input is unequal to that of another person (Carr & Valinezhad, 1994). Perceived inequity can result in low morale and reduced motivation to perform (Carr & Valinezhad, 1994). Social comparison theory is a variation on inequity theory that contends that individuals need to evaluate their opinions and abilities, and will choose others who have similar abilities and opinions as the basis for comparison (Carr & Valinezhad, 1994). Carr and Valinezhad conclude, "In the case of the CEO, the implication is that the compensation committee and the board of directors will anchor the CEO's compensation based on the constituent member's pay, or based on the pay of a CEO who is perceived to be similar or slightly better" (p. 90).

The free market economy is recognized as the major determinant of US wages throughout the firm (Wilhelm, 1993). Corporate boards that rely on the market to drive their decisions regarding CEO compensation often utilize comparative pay surveys (Wilhelm, 1993). There is some indication, however, that executive compensation surveys conducted by independent compensation consultants may be skewed upward because the companies that respond do not want to damage their future recruitment and retention efforts by being perceived as paying less competitive wages (Wilhelm, 1993).

CEO compensation is also impacted by the perceived competition for executive talent. Many corporate boards feel forced to pay the CEO an excessive salary regardless of the firm's performance to retain him or her in the role (Wilhelm, 1993). In fact, according to Tadelis (2002), it is the CEO who should be concerned about his or her future marketability in a competitive job market. Tadelis argues that the CEO must work hard to develop a solid performance record because the costs from damaging his or her reputation far exceed the benefits of poor performance. Wilhelm concludes that the corporate board:

> must recognize that surveys are bogus and CEO mobility is really low. Surveys presume that underpaid CEOs have many better-paying CEO jobs available to them. Openings are in fact scarce and many CEOs wouldn't be hired because their skills are limited mainly to one company or industry. Some CEOs are simply bureaucratic survivors and do not have demonstrable moneymaking power like the movie stars or professional athletes that they make invidious comparisons with. Higher pay has been argued as not necessary to entice people to head big companies. Plenty of qualified candidates would take the job even at half the pay. (p. 480)

Failure of Corporate Boards to Effectively Determine CEO Compensation

Power of the CEO

Managerial power is reflected in the degree to which the CEO can exert his or her will (Buchholtz et al., 1998). The corporate board was originally established to monitor and guide the firm, as well as to monitor and control the CEO, but many of today's boards lack the power when compared with that of the CEO to govern as they should (Wilhelm, 1993). Buchholtz et al. (1998) conclude that, "From a strong managerial power perspective, the board is an acquiescent rubber stamp co-opted by management" (p. 7).

There are several avenues by which a CEO may amass power that outstrips that of the corporate board. The more tenure that the CEO has in the firm, the more power he or she will have accumulated from a variety of sources (Buchholtz et al., 1998). Tenure affords the CEO the opportunity to build coalitions and a power base, and to establish credibility and influence with the board (Cordeiro & Veliyath, 2003). A tenured CEO may also develop expert power due to his or her knowledge of the inner workings of the firm (Buchholtz et al., 1998). The CEO's power and expertise increases the corporate board's dependence on him or her to provide the information that the board needs to govern the firm.

A CEO may also gain significant power relative to the corporate board if he or she is allowed to influence the selection of new board members (Cordeiro & Veliyath, 2003). The CEO may over time be able to stack the board with members who are beholden to him or her (Buchholtz et al., 1998). Board members not chosen by the CEO may also grow indebted to him or her if he or she uses his or her position of power to draw on firm resources to dispense benefits and favors to them (Buchholtz et al., 1998). Developing strong social relations is another means by which the CEO may gain power over the board (Buchholtz et al., 1998).

Another avenue by which a CEO may amass power is by influencing public opinion. Recent years have seen the emergence of the celebrity CEO, high-profile CEOs who are hailed as heroes in the business and the mainstream media (George, 2002). Too often, the granting of celebrity status to a CEO has had more to do with the CEO's wealth rather than success, and with his or her image and charisma rather than with demonstrated leadership ability (George, 2002). According to George, "We venerated the *flash in the pan* [italics added] while ignoring the real success stories because they are less dramatic and less glamorous" (p. 792).

Regardless of the source, once the CEO has gained power that outstrips that of the corporate board, the CEO is in a position to force action that maximizes his or her self-interests even if the action is at odds with the shareholders' interests (Buchholtz et al., 1998). Subsequently, a powerful CEO is more likely to influence the board to weaken any links between his or her pay and the firm's performance (Buchholtz et al., 1998).

Conflicts of Interest Between the Corporate Board and the CEO

One of the most significant sources of conflict of interest that may exist between a CEO and the corporate board occurs when the CEO also serves as the chairman of the board (Buchholtz et al., 1998). If the CEO serves in this dual role, he or she has the power to create the board's agenda, decide what information the board will receive, and control all discussions (Wilhelm, 1993). The CEO who serves in this dual role also has considerable influence over the selection of new board members, which has been earlier discussed as a source of great power for the CEO to force actions that maximizes his or her self-interests (Wilhelm, 1993; Buchholtz et al., 1998).

When the CEO is also the chairman of the board, the ability of the corporate board to objectively evaluate the CEO's work is significantly curtailed (Buchholtz et al., 1998). Also, according to Buchholtz et al. (1998), there is evidence that CEO duality is linked to managerial entrenchment devices such as greenmail, poison pills, and golden parachutes that tend to act against the best interests of the shareholders.

Conflicts of interest may also arise if some of the other members of the corporate board are also company insiders. Cordeiro and Veliyath (2003) state:

> Boards with a larger proportion of inside directors are more susceptible to being hand in glove with the CEO and the top management team. This increases the chance that the CEO's pay level will be disproportionately high, and out-of-line with firm performance as well as with external labor market norms. (p. 57)

Assessment of CEO's Performance

Determining appropriate CEO compensation is further complicated by the difficulty of accurately assessing the CEO's performance. The corporate board must determine if the weight of the assessment will be on the finance and accounting results generated by the firm under the CEO's leadership, the CEO's behavior, or some combination thereof (Ekanayake, 2004). Boards tend to favor result-focused assessments because it is much easier for the board to gather this data (Ekanayake, 2004). In recent years, however, attention has turned from traditional result measures such as growth, cash flow, and ROI; instead, the criterion for CEO performance has become meeting the expectations of security analysts (George, 2002).

CEOs are under considerable pressure from analysts and shareholders to continuously generate inordinately high short-term returns; companies that meet or exceed their earnings forecast are rewarded with higher stock prices, while those that do not may see a significant negative impact on their stock price, even if they record substantial earnings gains, and analysts may even call for the replacement of the CEO (George, 2002).

Add to this the fact that the CEO may also stand to profit from short-term boosts in the firm's stock price if part of his or her compensation includes stock or stock options, and one has created an environment that is ripe for ethical breaches. Because earnings and revenues cannot grow at a record pace year after year, the CEO may feel compelled to fudge or even fabricate financial data (George, 2002). The corporate board that is dependent on the CEO for information regarding the firm's performance may determine compensation based on flawed data. Accounting firms that traditionally could be trusted to provide the board with an objective assessment of the firm's financial picture may be biased in favor of the CEO because of the power the CEO wields to award lucrative consulting business to the accounting firm (George, 2002).

When the CEO's compensation is based only on the results reported in the accounting data, he or she has little incentive to take on projects that may secure the long-term health of the firm but do not have any immediate positive impact on returns (Ekanayake, 2004). It would be in the best interest of the shareholders if the corporate board included in its assessment of the CEO's performance some measures of actions the CEO is taking to secure the future of the firm.

Internal Compensation Committees

As designing the CEO's compensation package has become increasingly intricate, corporate boards have typically established a compensation committee, thereby allowing the complex issues involved in executive pay packages to be addressed in a smaller, more manageable group (Buchholtz et al., 1998). The committee may utilize comparable pay surveys and/or hire a compensation consultant to design the CEO compensation package, and then they present their recommended package to the board for final approval (Buchholtz et al., 1998).

One reason the compensation committee may make recommendations to the corporate board that provides excessive pay to the CEO is because the members of the committee are generally not objective. According to Buchholtz et al. (1998):

> The social dynamics between the CEO and the compensation committee present several opportunities for the CEO to bias the committee towards his or her pay preferences. For example, the directors may feel obligated to the CEO who recommends their cash compensation, stock options, and pensions to the committee for approval. Compensation Committee members who are highly paid may feel inclined to grant the CEO a generous pay package because it is comparable to their own. Also, committee members appointed after the CEO may feel that they are obligated to that CEO for having received their positions on the board. These arguments imply that the compensation committee member is a passive participant in a CEO-dominated pay-setting process. (p. 8)

Recommendations

Changes in Structure and Function of Corporate Boards

If corporate boards are to more effectively assess the CEO's performance and determine his or her compensation package, some changes in the common structure and function of the board, which will increase the board's power relative to the CEO, are essential. According to Buchholtz et al. (1998), a powerful board that has pervasive influence on the firm is critical to counter the CEO's power. Ideally, the board should establish a delicate balance between sharing leadership with the CEO and commanding power over the CEO as necessary (Buchholtz et al., 1998).

A powerful board does not necessarily imply that the board's relationship with the CEO will be adversarial (Buchholtz et al., 1998). The board should monitor and evaluate the firm's performance and be prepared to step in if they find a situation that requires immediate action, however, the board's role should most often be to provide support, encouragement, and expert counsel to the CEO (Buchholtz et al., 1998).

While cordial relations are important, if the board is to properly provide supervision, the relationship between the corporate board and the CEO should remain at arms length (Cordeiro & Veliyath, 2003). Cordeiro and Veliyath further recommend increasing the proportion of board members that are totally independent from the firm to increase the likelihood of arms-length relationships.

George (2002) concurs, suggesting that a minimum of 50 percent of the board members be independent, with 70 percent or more being ideal. Additionally, George states:

> We also need to tighten up the definition of "independence." Boards need directors who have had no prior association with the company as an employee or as an owner-employee of an acquired company. To insure their independence, no director should receive additional compensation other than standard board fees: no consulting fees, no speaking fees, no fees for doing business with the company, and no commissions on sales or acquisitions. Nor should any interlocking directorates be permitted between the CEO and any member of the board. (p. 5)

Another key to increasing the power of the corporate board is to prohibit CEO duality, that is, the CEO should not be permitted to also serve as the chairman of the board (George, 2002). Some have gone even further, suggesting that the CEO should not even be allowed to serve as a member of the board, nor should he or she have any role at all in the selection of new board members (Anonymous, 2003). Ideally, the board should be a completely independent committee of outsiders charged with setting expectations for the CEO's performance, objectively evaluating how effectively the CEO has performed against the expectations, and determining appropriate rewards based on the outcome of the performance evaluation.

When selecting new members, the corporate board should look for individuals who have some valuable expertise, strong awareness of the responsibilities associated with board membership, and the time to commit to board duties (Buchholtz et al., 1998). George (2002) agrees that time availability should be a requirement for board membership, arguing that there should be a limit to the number of boards with which an individual can participate at the same time.

Time to actively participate in the oversight process is important if the corporate board is to fulfill its fiduciary responsibilities to the fullest extent possible. The board must constantly question (1) not just if, but also how, the firm is achieving its results; (2) if the firm is making adequate investments for its long-term health; and (3) whether the firm's core strategies are still valid and being effectively implemented (George, 2002).

Specifically, in regards to the determination of the CEO's compensation package, changes should also be made to the compensation committee. Only board members who are completely independent from the firm should be allowed to participate in the compensation committee (Cordeiro & Veliyath, 2003). Other suggestions include utilizing a compensation consultant whose only connection to the firm is to work with the compensation committee to help them design a CEO compensation package that is clearly linked to key short- and long-term performance measures (Hardin et al., 1995), and prohibiting the CEO or any other member of management from participating in the compensation committee (George, 2002).

External Regulation of Corporate Boards

In the wake of recent high-profile examples of corporate boards' failure to fulfill their fiduciary responsibilities, many in the general public have called for legislation that would impose penalties on boards that fail to effectively govern. Strong government legislation that limits the compensation firms may pay their CEO is highly unlikely, nor do most experts believe that the government should make decisions on what companies can pay (Hardin et al., 1995). There are other outsiders, however, who should have some input into the design of the CEO's compensation package.

Currently, shareholders are legally prohibited from participating in setting CEO compensation because the Securities and Exchange Commission (SEC) views this activity as a part of ordinary business, and as such is outside of the realm of the shareholders' influence (Wilhelm, 1993). Organizations such as the United Shareholders Association and the American Shareholders Association are working to increase shareholder rights and participation in the governance process (Wilhelm, 1993). Wilhelm argues that shareholders should have the ability to elect their own representatives to sit on the corporate board, as well as to participate on the compensation committee.

Many large firms also have individuals or institutions that hold large blocks of stock (more than 5% of all outstanding shares) in the firm (Cordeiro & Veliyath, 2003). Cordeiro and Veliyath state that, "Since they have a larger investment at risk, these stockholders have a greater incentive and also the financial and legal ability to discipline inefficient managers and directors" (p. 58). The block stockholders should use their power to exert greater pressure on corporate boards to design CEO compensation packages that are a reasonable reflection of the CEO's performance, and that provide appropriate incentives for the CEO to act in the best interests of all shareholders.

Conclusion

One of the justifications offered for high CEO pay is the increased challenge of the CEO role due to factors, such as rapidly changing technology, hypercompetitive markets, and global business operations (Nichols & Subramaniam, 2001).

Ironically, these same factors may be used to support arguments on the harm that excessive CEO pay is having on the competitiveness of the US firms when compared with firms from countries in which average CEO pay is much less.

Wilhelm (1993) argues that excessive CEO pay is diverting funds from research and development (R&D) efforts, causing US firms to lag significantly behind their international counterparts in R&D spending. The competitive position of US firms is also hampered when CEOs load their firms with debt incurred from questionable growth (Wilhelm, 1993). As participation in the global economy grows increasingly important to firms' success, countries with average CEO pay that is significantly higher than elsewhere will be at a competitive disadvantage (Hardin et al., 1995).

Ultimately, it is the responsibility of the corporate board to ensure the firm's competitive viability for the sake of the shareholders. If excessive CEO pay is impeding the firm's competitiveness domestically as well as in global markets, the board has a fiduciary responsibility to act. Implementing some of the recommendations noted in this chapter may support the board in structuring a compensation package that provides the CEO with adequate incentives to act in the best short- and long-term interests of the firm.

REFERENCES

Alam, P., Arora, A., and Pearson, M. A. 2000. Enhancing the quality of CEO compensation disclosures. *The Mid-Atlantic Journal of Business*, **36**(1): 7–15.

Anonymous. 2003. Corporate governance: corporate integrity. *Vital Speeches of the Day*, **69**(19): 596–601.

Beauchamp, T. L. and Bowie, N. E. 2004. *Ethical Theory and Business*, 7th edn. Upper Saddle River, NJ: Prentice-Hall.

Bruhl, R. H. 2003. A possible solution to the principal-agent problem posed by the contemporary corporate CEO. *Journal of Business Ethics*, **48**(4): 401–402.

Buchholtz, A. K., Young, M. N., and Powell, G. N. 1998. Are board members pawns or watchdogs? The link between CEO pay and firm performance. *Group & Organization Management*, **23**(1): 6–26.

Carr, L. L. and Valinezhad, M. 1994. The role of ethics in executive compensation: toward a contractarian interpretation of the neoclassical theory of managerial renumeration. *Journal of Business Ethics*, **13**(2): 81–97.

Cordeiro, J. J. and Veliyath, R. 2003. Beyond pay for performance: a panel study of the determinants of CEO compensation. *American Business Review*, **21**(1): 56–66.

Ekanayake, S. 2004. Agency theory, national culture and management control systems. *Journal of American Academy of Business, Cambridge*, **4**(1 / 2): 49–54.

Gago, S. and Rodgers, W. 2003. A model for capturing ethics and executive compensation. *Journal of Business Ethics*, **48**(2): 189–202.

George, W. W. 2002. Restoring governance to our corporations: crisis in the corporate world. *Vital Speeches of the Day*, **68**(24): 791–796.

Hardin, T., Schick, J., and Walters, B. 1995. What should top executives be paid? *Human Resource Management International Digest*, **3**(4): 4–6.

Nichols, D. and Subramaniam, C. 2001. Executive compensation: excessive or equitable? *Journal of Business Ethics*, **29**(4): 339–351.

Tadelis, S. 2002. The market for reputations as an incentive mechanism. *The Journal of Political Economy*, **110**(4), 854–882.

Wilhelm, P. G. 1993. Application of distributive justice theory to the CEO pay problem: recommendations for reform. *Journal of Business Ethics*, **12**(6): 469–482.

9

Executive Pay in Public Academia: A Non-Justice-Based Argument for the Reallocation of Compensation

James Stacey Taylor
Department of Philosophy and Religious Studies, The College of New Jersey, Ewing, NJ 08628

One of the perennial complaints of academics is that their salaries are too low for the level of education that they have achieved. In recent years this complaint has been voiced more stridently as the salaries of top academic administrators at public institutions have started to rival those of their counterparts in the business world. In 2002, for example, the revelation that the Chancellor of Louisiana State University had received a pay raise from $205,000 to $490,000 led to a vociferous national debate concerning the level of compensation that it was ethical to pay to academic executives. This debate was further fuelled by an article in the *Chronicle of Higher Education* that outlined the salaries that are paid to the best-compensated senior executives of public (and private) universities in the United States (Basinger, 2003).

The debate over the ethics of the level of compensation paid to many senior executives at public universities mirrors that over the salary levels of their counterparts in the business world. Despite this, little attention has been paid to the ethics of executive compensation within the ivory tower compared to that lavished on its equivalent in the corporate jungle. Indeed, as recently as in 2001 Nichols and Subramaniam were able truthfully to write that the issue of high levels of compensation in fields other than business "has received almost no attention or outcry." In part, this might be because the salary levels that are enjoyed by the most highly paid executives in academia are low in comparison to those paid to their corporate cousins. It is far easier to become outraged over

---

Paper presented at the 2004 Japha Symposium on Business and Professional Ethics on "The Ethics of Executive Compensation."

compensation packages totalling $102.45 million (Lawrence Coss of Green Tree Financial), $97.59 million (Anthony Grove of Intel), or $94.16 million (Sanford Weill of Traveler's group) than it is to become outraged at salaries "closing in on $1 million," to quote the title of the above-mentioned article in *The Chronicle of Higher Education*.[1] Yet irrespective of the reasons that lie behind this oversight, it is unfortunate. Most obviously, this is because the issue of executive compensation with academia is worthy of ethical examination in its own right. Moreover, the focus of the discussion of the ethics of executive compensation in academia differs in two important respects from that of the discussion of corporate compensation. First, owing to the way in which most public universities are funded the competition for compensation between their employees is a zero-sum game.[2] This is not necessarily true for private firms, whose executives' efforts could add more incremental income to the company than is paid out in their salaries. In such cases, the other employees of the company might receive higher salaries than they would, were the executives in question not to work for their employer. Second, the primary aim of public institutions of higher education is to enhance personal autonomy,[3] where the primary (or even, perhaps, the sole) aim of most private firms is profit (Friedman, 1970).

These two differences between executive compensation in the setting of a public institution of higher education and executive compensation in the setting of a private firm set the background for the argument that will be developed in this chapter. This argument will favor reallocating resources away from the highly paid executives of public academic institutions of higher education, and toward (in part) their lower-paid colleagues. Unlike most pro-reallocation arguments that are developed in the debate over the ethics of executive compensation, this argument will not be based on noting that there is a large disparity between the compensation paid to university executives and other university employees.[4] Nor will it be based on noting that the compensation gap between the average university employee and university executives is widening,[5] or the claim that university

---

[1] The cited figures are quoted by Nichols and Subramaniam, 2001: 304.

[2] Empirical evidence for this is given in Warner Chris, 2004. This paper was published on the website of the LSU branch of the American Association for University Professors.

[3] That the aim of education is the fostering of personal autonomy is noted by Paterson, 1996: 1–16 and Deardon, 1972: 448–465.

[4] For an expression of this view concernine the ethics of executive compensation in the corporate world see, for example, Rheingold, Jennifer (1997).

[5] For example, Martin Sabo, a Minnesota Congressman, between 1991 and 2001 introduced bills to disallow tax deductions for executive salaries in excess of 25 times the salary of the lowest paid

executives are overpaid relative to the other employees at their universities given the amount of work each group performs.[6] Instead, this argument will be based on noting that one of the primary aims of a public institution of higher education is to enhance personal autonomy. With this in hand it will be argued that since relatively small increases in the level of compensation afforded to a university's lower-level employees would result in a significant increase in their ability to exercise their autonomy, not to provide them with such increases would be incommensurate with one of the primary aims of the university concerned.[7] Given the zero-sum nature of the funding of employee compensation at public universities, then, the lower-level employees of such institutions should receive a salary increase taken from the compensation packages of their executives. Since this resource reallocation is required with respect to the primary aim of the institutions concerned, were their financial administrators not to engage in it, they would fail to discharge their fiduciary responsibilities. Such administrators are thus morally required to reallocate compensatory resources from their institutions' executives to their lower-paid employees.

Setting the Stage

It must be emphasized that the argument in this chapter is a conditional argument of the form, "If autonomy is the primary end of public higher education, then the current levels of compensation that are enjoyed by the executives of public institutions of higher education are too high, and should be reallocated to such institutions' lower-paid employees." The argument will thus be unpersuasive to persons who believe that the enhancement of autonomy is not the primary aim of higher education. There are two possible responses to this initial worry. First, since the view that the enhancement of autonomy is not one of the ends of higher education is a distinctly minority one, the argument advanced

---

employee in the same firm, on the grounds that such disparity is immoral. (Noted by Nichols and Subramaniam, 2001: 342). In the context of pay raises for academic administrators see Rau and Bell, 2004. This paper was published on the website of the LSU branch of the American Association for University Professors.

[6] See Perel Mel (2003) and Rodgers Waymond and Gago Susana (2003). This type of argument was also noted by Nichols and Subramaniam (2001: 344).

[7] Of course, this is provided that such an increase in the exercise of their autonomy could be achieved with no net diminution of the enjoyment of such exercise overall.

in this chapter will be of interest to most of the participants in the debate over executive pay in higher education. Second, the argument does not rest on the individual accepting that the enhancement of autonomy is the primary aim of public higher education. This argument could be adapted for any alternative aim that one might believe is the primary aim of higher education, such as the fostering of human well being, or the advancement of knowledge. If one believes that public higher education has such an alternative aim, then one need only to alter the antecedent clause of the above conditional argument to reflect one's beliefs, and then adapt this argument to argue in favor of the reallocation of executive compensation in the direction that one prefers. In a related vein, it should be noted that the view that the primary aim of public institutions of higher education is the enhancement of autonomy does not rest on any particular account of autonomy. Since this is so, the arguments in this chapter will similarly be agnostic as to which account of autonomy is correct. They will thus be acceptable to autonomy theorists of all stripes.[8] More particularly, although most educational theorists write of higher education (and education in general) "enhancing" the autonomy of those who receive it, the autonomy-based argument in this chapter will eschew this typical view. Instead, the argument will focus on higher education's aim to enable persons to *exercise* their autonomy more effectively, rather than on the more general claim that it can enhance persons' autonomy *per se*. Moreover, the argument will not solely focus on the ability of an institute of higher education to enhance the autonomy of those who attend it as students. Rather, it will be argued that since the aim of such institutions is to enable persons to exercise their autonomy more effectively, they should do so for *everyone* affiliated with them: students, professors, administrators, and all their support staff. Finally, since the arguments in this chapter are directed to a genuine moral problem of what academics like to call the "real world" it will be assumed that persons whose incomes are in question are neither "utility monsters" nor ascetics. That is, it will be assumed that it is not the case that every increase in a person's income will yield an equal benefit to him in terms of his ability to exercise his autonomy, nor is it the case that a person's desires and goals are such that the amount of resources that he has at his disposal is irrelevant to his ability to satisfy or achieve them.

---

[8] Thus, the arguments in this paper will be agnostic between the different theories of autonomy that are outlined in James Stacey Taylor, 2005.

The Argument in Brief - and Three Initial Clarifications

Before moving to outline in full the argument for the reallocation of the salaries of highly paid executives of public institutions of higher education it would be useful to outline it in brief, and then to clarify it in three important respects to prevent it from being misunderstood.

The argument below will be based on the view that the primary aim of higher education is to foster the exercise of autonomy. This premise will then be joined by a second, that the reallocation of compensation from highly paid executives to lower paid employees will achieve this aim by enabling the latter to exercise their autonomy to an additional degree that would be greater than any consequent diminution in the ability of the former to exercise theirs. Thus, this argument concludes, if the primary aim of an institute of higher education is to foster autonomy, were its administrators not to engage in such reallocation, they would be acting against the purpose of the institution that employs them. And since this would be a breach of their fiduciary relationship to such institutions, such a failure to reallocate would be immoral.

This argument bears a strong resemblance to arguments that are offered to show that persons who work in very low-paid jobs in the corporate world (e.g., in sweatshops) should receive more compensation for their efforts, and that this additional compensation should be taken from the salaries of the highly paid executives of the companies that employ them. The pro-reallocation argument that is offered here, however, differs in important respects from such (more common) arguments in important respects. The arguments that are offered in favor of redistributing the compensation that is paid to executives in private firms to their lower-paid colleagues are often couched in terms of whether the lower-paid persons should be allowed to undertake certain forms of employment (e.g., sweatshop labor) for certain levels of compensation. That is, these arguments typically focus on the question of whether it is morally permissible paternalistically to restrict the actions of potential low-paid employees by preventing them from accepting such employment. This way of framing the debate over the morality of the reallocation of executive compensation from highly paid executives to their lower paid colleagues places the onus firmly upon the proponents of such reallocation to explain why the activities of these potential employees should be so restricted. Such an explanation is hard to provide. This is especially so where it would be the case that the potential low-paid employees would be made better off (including better off with respect to the exercise of their autonomy) by accepting the employment they are offered. But this way of framing the debate over the reallocation of executive compensation when discussing the ethics of executive compensation in public academia is misleading. The issue in this context is *not* whether the potential lower-paid employees should be paternalistically protected from their own choices. Rather, the issue is whether to protect them from the choices of *others*, namely, those institutional administrators who are offering them employment at pre-reallocation (i.e., current) rates. The focus of this argument in favor of the reallocation of compensation in public academia is thus explicitly on the question of *whether persons who offer others employment at pre-reallocation (i.e., current) levels of compensation do anything morally wrong*. And, in the context of the debate over the reallocation of compensatory resources in public academia, the question of whether these persons would do anything morally wrong by failing to reallocate turns on the issue of whether such reallocation is required with respect to autonomy.

This first clarification of the following pro-redistribution argument leads to the second. The question of whether the financial administrators of public institutions of higher education who offer employment without reallocating resources from the institution's executives to its lower paid employees thereby act wrongly is broader than the question of whether this would lead to the autonomy of the persons offered (and accepting) such employment being *impaired*. This is because it is possible for a person to make offers to others that, from the point of view of one who prizes autonomy, are morally impermissible as they evince a less than morally appropriate evaluation of the autonomy of the persons to whom they are made. Such an attitude could be evinced even if these persons' acceptance of these offers would make them *better off* with respect to their autonomy. For example, someone who comes across a drowning person and offers to save him if, and only if, he becomes her personal slave, would, if he accepts the offer and she fulfils her promise, make him better off with respect to his enjoyment of autonomy. However, by enslaving him she would not have responded appropriately to the value of his autonomy. Rather, she would have evinced a morally inappropriate attitude toward it. Since offers that evince a morally inappropriate view of another's autonomy are, from the point of view of one who values autonomy, morally impermissible, it is possible that a university's offer of employment to a (potentially) low paid employee might similarly be impermissible insofar as it evinces a less than morally appropriate evaluation of his autonomy. And this could be so *even if* the lower-paid employee's acceptance of this offer would make him *better off* with respect to his exercise of autonomy.

This second point of clarification leads to the final one: what is meant by "a less than morally appropriate evaluation of autonomy." At first sight it might appear that the proponents of any argument that is based upon a claim concerning the value of personal autonomy must provide some indication of its value, for otherwise they will be unable to say with certainty when a person's autonomy has been "less than appropriately valued." Yet although this argument for reallocation appeals to a view of the appropriate value of autonomy, it can progress *without* a positive account of the value of autonomy. The purpose in invoking the value of autonomy in this argument is solely to establish that *in the eyes of those who hold the fostering of autonomy to be the primary aim of higher education* a failure to redistribute compensation from highly paid executives to their lower paid colleagues would impermissibly undervalue the latter's autonomy. Of course, without a positive account of the value of personal autonomy the conclusion of this pro-redistribution argument is limited in its practical applicability, for without such an account one could not identify which public institutions of higher education are compensating their employees in a moral manner and which are not.[9] Yet this limitation will not undermine the overall thrust of the argument below, whose aim is to show that respect for autonomy justifies the reallocation of executive compensation – and that there are clear cases where such reallocation is morally required.

Why Respect for Autonomy Requires the Reallocation of Compensation

With the above three clarifications in place it is time to develop the argument for the reallocation of compensation away from the highly paid executives of public academic institutions to their lower-paid colleagues. The first premise of this argument is that public institutions of higher education have a set amount of funding allocated to them each year by the States that support them. The distribution of the funds allocated is thus a zero-sum game. That is, if a person or department X receives N amount of funds from the total T, then person or department Y has to share (T minus N) funds with the other persons or departments apart from X that receive their funding from the same source. The degree

---

[9] Moreover, the value of autonomy is unlikely to be amenable to precise quantification – and even if it were, there are obvious epistemological problems associated with assessing how much autonomy a person enjoys, and how much he could have enjoyed had he been treated differently.

of compensation that a university executive receives from the funds allotted to her institution thus reduces the amount that is available for other uses, such as salary for her colleagues. The second premise of this argument for reallocation is that most persons are able to exercise their autonomy more effectively (i.e., they are able to do more) if they have more resources available to them.[10] Thus, a person who earns $10 per hour is better able to direct himself as he chooses, and so better able to exercise his autonomy, than a person who earns only $5 an hour, for the lesser resources possessed by the latter person will limit the number of viable options that are open to him. Increasing the amount of resources that a person has access to will not, however, proportionately increase his ability to exercise his autonomy, for as a person's resources increase he will receive diminishing returns from them with respect to the exercise of his autonomy. For example, increasing a person's yearly wage from $10,000 to $20,000 is likely dramatically to increase the number of viable options that he can now choose from, and so is likely dramatically to increase his ability to direct his own life, to exercise his autonomy, to satisfy his desires, and pursue his goals. Yet increasing a wealthy person's yearly wage by the same amount (e.g., from $490,000 to $500,000) will have a negligible effect on her ability to direct her life, to exercise her autonomy. Thus, since a wealthy person's ability to exercise her autonomy would only be marginally improved (if it will be improved at all) by an increase in her salary, the diminution in a wealthy person's ability to exercise her autonomy would similarly only be marginally affected were her income to fall by the same amount (i.e., if she were to suffer a drop in income of the same amount that, were she to receive this through a raise in income, would result in only a marginal increase in her ability to exercise her autonomy). Conversely, a lower-paid employee's ability to exercise his autonomy would increase dramatically were he to receive as a raise the amount of income that would only minimally adversely affect the ability of the wealthier employee to exercise her autonomy were she to suffer its loss.

When these two premises (that public universities receive a fixed income, whose allocation results in a zero-sum game for its potential recipients, and that persons receive diminishing marginal returns with respect to the increase in their abilities to exercise their autonomy the higher their incomes are) are combined

---

[10] This is true for "most" persons because whether a person is better able to exercise his autonomy with more resources will depend upon his particular desires and goals. If a person's desires and goals are such that he does not need any resources to satisfy or accomplish them, this claim will not be true.

with the premise that the fostering of the exercise of autonomy is the primary aim of an institute of higher education, the argument in favor of reallocating the salaries paid to its wealthy executives is straightforward, namely the primary end of an institution of higher education is the fostering of autonomy. The resources that have been allocated to it should thus be distributed so as to maximize the fostering of autonomy. Increasing a person's salary will have a greater effect on her ability to exercise her autonomy the lower her current salary is. Since this is so, any salary increases that are made by the institution should be directed first to its lower paid employees, and then to employees further up the salary scale. Moreover, reducing the salaries of the highest-paid employees would only have a marginal effect on their ability to exercise their autonomy, while correlatively increasing the salaries of the lowest-paid employees would have a significant and positive effect on their abilities to exercise their autonomy. Hence, insofar as an institution of higher education aims at the fostering of the exercise of autonomy, its financial administrators should reallocate significant portions of the salaries of its highest paid employees to its lower paid employees. Thus, the financial administrators of a public institution of higher education who pay its senior executives large salaries and fail to reallocate their incomes to its lower-paid employees are acting contrary to the aim of the institution that employs them. And such a breach of their fiduciary responsibility is immoral.

An Autonomy-Based Objection to Reallocation – and Responses to it

The Argument

Although it might appear from the above argument that persons who believe that the primary aim of public institutes of higher education is to foster autonomy should favor the reallocation of the compensation of the executives of such institutions, to concur with this conclusion might be too hasty. This is because instead of being *required* by respect for autonomy, and thus being required by respect for the primary aim of such institutions, the reallocation of the compensatory resources of such institutions in this way might instead evince a *failure* to respect autonomy. And, if so, such reallocation would lead to a failure to act in accord with such institutions' aims.

This autonomy-based objection to the above argument for reallocation is based on changing the focus of the debate from the question of whether the administrators of public institutions of higher education may make certain offers of employment to potentially low paid employees, to the question of whether a respecter of autonomy may legitimately advocate curtailing the autonomy of these potential employees. The proponent of this autonomy-based objection notes that if it is wrong for an administrator of a public institution of higher education to make an offer of employment to a potential low paid employee, then it would be better, were he not to do this – even if this meant the potential employee in question would thus not receive this job offer. That is, the proponent of this objection notes, the above argument for reallocation requires that the potential employees of public institutions of higher education be prevented from accepting employment from such institutions in the absence of such reallocation. But this is counterintuitive in two respects. First, if accepting the job in question would enhance the autonomy of the recipient, it seems that one who values autonomy should favor the job being offered to the potential employee, not oppose it. Second, in claiming that it would be wrong for an administrator to offer such a job to a potential employee one is claiming that the potential employee's autonomy should be curtailed for his own good. (That is, one is claiming that he should not be able to exercise his autonomy by accepting such a job, for he should not act in a way that supports a system of job offers that evinces a morally impermissible under evaluation of his autonomy.) But this seems highly paternalistic, for it imposes upon the employees whose actions it restricts an evaluation of their own autonomy (i.e., it is valuable enough so that its fostering should be the primary aim of a public institution of higher education) that they might not share. Since one who genuinely prizes autonomy should not readily countenance such interference with the autonomous decisions and actions of others, it seems that the above argument in favor of reallocation is not one that a defender of autonomy can consistently make.

The Responses to This Objection

A proponent of the above argument for reallocation has, however, a response to each of these seemingly counterintuitive results. In response to the first, she would note that the rightness or wrongness of an action is a *scalar* property. That is, acts differ in the degree to which they are right or wrong. This being so, then whereas it would be morally wrong for an administrator of a public institution of higher education to offer employment to a low paid employee in a situation where the compensation of the institution's highly paid executives was not reallocated, it would be morally *worse* for no such offers to be made.[11] In response to the second of the apparently counterintuitive results outlined above, the proponent of the above argument for reallocation could note that one who values autonomy can accept that a person can suffer a *local* diminution in his exercise of autonomy (e.g., he is prevented from accepting a low paid job to ensure that he accepts one that is more highly paid) where this is suffered in order to ensure that he receive a *global* increase in his ability to exercise his autonomy if he agrees to this.[12] Since, if asked, the employees whose exercise of autonomy would be restricted, were the administrators to adhere to the moral standards imposed by the proponents of the argument for reallocation would agree to have their autonomy compromised in this way (i.e., they would agree to have their potential salaries raised), this restriction of the exercise of their autonomy would be acceptable to a respecter of autonomy.

A Counter to the Second Response – and a Final Reply

Yet although the first of the above responses that the proponent of the above argument for reallocation might make to the above objection is plausible, the second is likely to give pause to persons familiar with the debate over the moral legitimacy of paternalism. This is because this response is that which the defenders of paternalism often resort to in order to justify the imposition of their views upon others, and so does not appear to be one that a person who values autonomy highly should readily invoke. Despite this, however, a person who values autonomy highly *can* legitimately claim that the redistribution of compensation that is required by the argument for reallocation does not impermissibly restrict the autonomy of the potential employees who would be affected by it. This is because, she could claim, the (typical) potential low paid employee (whether in public academia or elsewhere) will not autonomously desire *simpliciter* to

---

[11] Note that the issue of a morality of a situation is distinct from the issue of whether the actors in that situation are praiseworthy or blameworthy. Thus, a proponent of the above argument for reallocation could hold that it would be morally worse for no offers of employment to be made to (potential) low paid employees than for such offers to be made, without thereby holding the administrators who would otherwise be making such offers blameworthy for their failure to do so. They might, for example, be failing to offer employment, as they do not have the funds to do so.

[12] The difference between global and local diminutions and enhancements of autonomy is outlined in Dworkin Gerald, 1988.

contract for a low paid job. Instead, he would only autonomously desire to enter into these contracts because of the (impoverished) situation that he is in. Since he would prefer not to be in such a deprived situation, the typical potential low paid employee would prefer not to act on his desire to enter into these contracts. Instead, he would prefer to be in a situation where acting on this desire is not likely to be the best course of action for him to pursue. The implicit claim that this second counterintuitive result rests on (that, were the argument from reallocation's conclusion to be enforced, it would interfere with the potential employees' exercise of their autonomy in pursuit of their autonomous preferences), thus importantly under describes the situations of these potential employees. The restrictions on the actions of the potential low paid employees that would be required, were the conclusion of this pro-reallocation argument to be implemented, would not prevent such potential employees from doing what they really want to do, as this objection to regulation implies (Kip Viscusi, 1983). Instead, such restriction would merely substitute an option that is more preferable from the point of view of the typical potential employee for one that he considers to be less preferable. Restricting the potential low paid employees of public institutions of higher education from accepting jobs at a low rate of compensation would thus, from the point of view of the potential low paid employee, *increase*, not decrease, the instrumental value of his autonomy to him. Accordingly, the restrictions that would be placed on such a person's exercise of his autonomy, were the conclusion of the pro-reallocation argument to be implemented, would not run afoul of the moral requirement to respect his autonomy. Indeed, they are actually *required* by it.

Conclusion

So far, the focus of this chapter has been on the reallocation of compensation from one group of employees within a public institution of higher education (i.e., highly paid executives) to another (their lower-paid colleagues). The conclusion of this pro-reallocation argument is not, however, simply that respect for autonomy requires that resources be reallocated among the employees of such institutions. Rather, the conclusion of the above argument is that resources should be reallocated away from the highly paid executives of public institutions of higher education *when this would serve to foster the exercise of autonomy*. Such resources should thus not only be reallocated to these executives' lower-paid colleagues, but also into *other* avenues where their use would serve better to foster autonomy.

They could, for example, be reallocated to provide scholarships to enable students to attend the academic institution, who would not have otherwise been able to do so, or to fund research in areas where advances in knowledge would foster autonomy (e.g., medicine). Rather than merely supporting the reallocation of resources from one group of employees of public academic institutions to another group, then, the above argument supports a *broader* conclusion that such resources should be reallocated to wherever they would best be employed in fostering the exercise of autonomy.

Yet if the conclusion of the above argument for reallocation is broader than the focus of this chapter so far might suggest, its scope is also *narrower* than it might appear at first. The above argument for reallocation is based on the premise that the allocation of resources within a public academic institution is a zero-sum game, and so if resources are used to compensate such an institution's executives then they will not be available for other uses. Yet although this is frequently true with respect to the resources that are provided to institutions of public education by the States that support them, it is also true that the compensation that is paid to many top executives in such institutions is in many cases a *mixture* of private and public funds. And the argument for reallocation that is offered here does not support the conclusion that the compensation that is paid to the executives of public institutions of higher education from private funds should similarly be reallocated. This is for two reasons. First, the allocation of such funds to the executives concerned does not thereby necessarily deprive any other constituents of their employing institution of their use. Second, the above argument for reallocation was based on the premise that the primary purpose of a public institute of higher education was the fostering of autonomy. This premise does not necessarily hold with respect to the private foundations or organizations whose members might choose to supplement the compensation that is paid to the executives of such institutions. Were such organizations to provide such executives with additional compensation rather than allocating their funds to foster the development of autonomy, then, they would not necessarily be acting against their own stated purposes, as would the institutions, were they to act in this way. As such, then, whereas the financial administrators of public institutions of higher education would be violating their fiduciary duties, were they to allocate their resources in this way, the administrators of the private organizations who might choose to supplement the salaries of the institutions' executives would not necessarily do so. Thus, whereas such allocation of resources would be an immoral one for the administrators of public institutions of higher education to agree upon, it would not be immoral for the former persons to utilize it.

This latter observation leads to the final point of this chapter, that the above argument for reallocation cannot be readily generalized to provide an argument for the reallocation of resources in any organization *but* a public institution of higher education. The above argument for reallocation is based on the premise that one of the primary aims of such an institution is the fostering of the exercise of autonomy – and, as was noted in the introduction to this chapter, this aim is not necessarily shared by other organizations. Of course, one could argue that the above argument should be generalized on the grounds that autonomy is of such great moral value that all organizations have a *prima facie* obligation to promote its exercise. But such an argument is beyond the scope of this chapter.

REFERENCES

Basinger Julianne. 2003. Closing in on $1 million. *The Chronicle of Higher Education*, **50**: S1, November 14th.

Deardon, R. F. 1972. Autonomy and education. In R. F. Deardon, P. H. Hirst, and R. S. Peters, eds., *Education and the Development of Reason*. London: Routledge and Kegan Paul.

Dworkin Gerald. 1988. *The Theory and Practice of Autonomy*. Cambridge: Cambridge University Press, p. 25.

Friedman Milton. 1970. The social responsibility of business is to increase its profits. *New York Times Magazine*, September 13th.

James Stacey Taylor. 2005. Introduction. In James Stacey Taylor, ed., *Personal Autonomy: New Essays on Personal Autonomy and its Role in Contemporary Moral Philosophy*. Cambridge: Cambridge University Press.

Nichols Donald and Subramaniam Chandra. 2001. Executive compensation: excessive or equitable? *Journal of Business Ethics*, **29**: 345.

Paterson, R. W. K. 1996. Education and autonomy. In John Wallis, ed., *Liberal Adult Education: The End of an Era?* Nottingham, UK: Continuing Education Press.

Perel Mel. 2003. An ethical perspective on CEO compensation. *Journal of Business Ethics*, **48**: 381–391.

Rau Ravi A. P. and Bell Paul. 2004. Infectious greed, at: http://www.bus.lsu.edu/accounting/faculty/lcrumbley/InfectGreed.htm#infgreedgraph1, accessed August 21, 2004.

Rheingold Jennifer. 1997. Executive pay. *Business Week*, April 12. 58–66.

Rodgers Waymond and Gago Susana. 2003. A model capturing ethics and executive compensation. *Journal of Business Ethics*, **48**: 189–202.

Viscusi W. Kip. 1983. *Risk By Choice: Regulating Health and Safety in the Workplace*. Cambridge, MA: Harvard University Press, p. 80.

Warner Chris. 2004. Business as usual at LSU, http://www.bus.lsu.edu/accounting/faculty/lcrumbley/Businessatlsu2.html, accessed August 21, 2004.

10

How to (Try to) Justify CEO Pay

Jeffrey Moriarty
Department of Philosophy, Bowling Green State University

America's corporate executives get paid huge sums of money. *Business Week* estimates that, in 2003, CEOs of the 365 largest US corporations were paid on average $8 million, 301 times as much as factory workers (Lavelle, 2004). CEOs' pay packages, including salary, bonus, and restricted stock and stock option grants, increased by 340 percent from 1991 to 2001, while workers' paychecks increased by only 36 percent (Byrne, 2002). What, if anything, is wrong with this?

Although it has received a great deal of attention in management and economics journals and in the popular press, the topic of executive compensation has been virtually ignored by philosophers. As a result, its normative dimensions have been largely ignored. Organizational theorists and economists tend to be more interested in what the determinants of CEO pay *are* than in what they *should be*.[1] What is needed, I suggest, is a general ethical framework for thinking about justice in pay. The following section elaborates this framework, which is then used in the rest of the chapter to argue that CEOs get paid too much.

Three Views of Justice in Wages

To determine whether CEOs get paid too much, we first need to consider what, in general, makes a wage just. In this section, I will sketch three views of justice in wages, each of which is based on a widely recognized moral value. I do not claim that these are the only views of justice in wages possible. But the values from which they derive are the ones most frequently appealed to in the debates about CEO pay. It is unlikely that any other view would be as attractive.

This chapter first appeared in a longer version as Do CEOs get paid too much? in *Business Ethics Quarterly*, **15** (2005): 257–281. It is reprinted here with kind permission of the Society for Business Ethics and the Philosophy Documentation Center.

[1] I will focus on the pay of CEOs. But my conclusions apply, other things equal, to the pay of other top executives.

According to what I will call the "agreement view," just prices for goods are obtained through arm's-length negotiations between informed buyers and informed sellers (Crystal, 1991). In our case, the goods are the CEO's services, the seller is the CEO, and the buyer(s) is (are) the company's owner(s). Provided there are no imperfections (e.g., fraud, coercion) in the bargaining process, the agreement view says, the wage that comes out of it is just. Owners are free to do what they want with their money, and CEOs are free to do what they want with their services.

The "desert view" appeals to independent standards for justice in wages. It says that people deserve certain wages for performing certain jobs, whatever they might agree to accept for performing them. The wages people deserve may depend on facts about their jobs (e.g., their difficulty or degree of responsibility), people's performances in them (e.g., how much effort they expend, how much they contribute to the firm), or both. According to the desert view, the CEO should be paid $8 million per year if and only if he deserves to be paid $8 million per year.

What I will call the "utility view" conceives of wages not as rewards for past work, but as incentives for future work. The purpose of wages on this view is to maximize firm wealth by attracting, retaining, and motivating talented workers. If, in our case, the CEO's position is not compensated adequately, few talented candidates will apply or remain on the job for long, and the company as a whole will suffer. On the other hand, an expensive CEO can easily earn his keep through even small increases in the price of the company's stock. According to the utility view, then, a compensation package of $8 million per year is just if and only if it maximizes firm wealth by attracting, retaining, and optimally motivating a talented CEO.[2]

Too often in discussions of executive compensation, the separateness of these views is overlooked. But if we do not distinguish among them, we run the risk of talking past each other. P's belief that CEOs do not deserve, by any standard of deservingness, $8 million per year may lead him to the concluion that CEOs make too much money. Q's belief that the pay negotiations between CEOs and

---

[2] Some might deny that it makes sense to speak of an "agreement view" or "utility view" of *justice* in wages. We can talk about whether utility or agreements should determine the wages workers get all-things-considered. But, according to this objection, justice is *defined* in terms of desert; the just wage, by definition, is the wage the worker deserves. I do not want to engage in a terminological dispute. What the objection describes as a debate about the wages workers should get all-things-considered *just is* what I describe as a debate about justice in wages.

owners are fair, may lead him to conclude that CEOs do not make too much money. In fact, both P and Q may agree that CEOs do not deserve $8 million per year and that the pay negotiations between CEOs and owners are fair. They may simply disagree about what is morally more important: deserts or agreements. Understanding this, of course, does not solve the debate. But it does help to clarify what it might be about.

To solve the debate about CEO pay, we must determine which view of justice in wages is correct. It is unlikely (for reasons given below) that agreement-theorists, desert-theorists, and utility-theorists will all come to the same conclusion about how much CEOs should be paid. I will not try to do this here. There is deep disagreement about the relative importance of these values. A full defense of one of them against the others is beyond the scope of this chapter. Fortunately, it is not necessary to determine which view of justice in wages is correct to draw *any* conclusions about CEO pay. Below I will argue that its current level cannot be justified by the agreement view, the desert view, or the utility view. No matter which one is correct, CEOs get paid too much. It is possible, as I indicated, that new theories of justice in wages could be developed. But the theories we have sketched are based on the most common moral values, and it is not at all clear what these new theories would look like. Until it is, we have reason to believe that the current level of CEO pay cannot be justified *simpliciter*.

The Agreement View

According to this view, a just price for the CEO's services is one that results from an arm's-length negotiation between an informed CEO and informed owners. I will show that these negotiations are not, in general, conducted at arm's-length. If they were, CEOs would be paid on average less than $8 million per year.[3]

The problem occurs mainly on the "buy" side of the equation, so we will focus our attention there. Traditionally, shareholders are represented in negotiations with the CEO by a subset of the members of the company's board of directors. This may seem promising to those who would appeal to the agreement view to justify the current level of CEO compensation. Since directors are elected by

---

[3] More precisely, CEOs would be paid *on average* less than $8 million per year. It is possible that some CEOs are not overpaid according to any of the three views of justice in wages. But even if some – or as I suspect, most – are, it follows that average CEO pay is too high.

shareholders, they might say, it is likely that the directors who negotiate with the CEO – those who form the board's "compensation committee" – are in fact independent and informed. If shareholders did not elect independent and informed directors, they would risk paying too much to an incompetent CEO, or too little to an exceptional one.

This hope is unfounded. It is well known that shareholders do not, in fact, elect directors in any meaningful way. When a seat on the board opens up, usually there is just one person who "runs" in the "election." Once a candidate is nominated, her election is a formality. The group that controls the nomination process, then, controls the board's membership. In most cases, this is not the shareholders but the board itself, whose chairman in 84% of American firms is the firm's CEO (Shivdasani & Yermack, 1999; Nichols & Subramanian, 2001). Although there has been a trend away from direct CEO involvement in the nominating process in recent years (Shivdasani & Yermack, 1999), most CEOs still wield considerable informal influence over it (O'Reilly et al., 1988; Main et al., 1995).

This is worrisome. Whereas shareholders may elect, out of apathy or ignorance, directors who are unfamiliar with the industry and friendly with the CEO, CEOs can encourage the appointment of such directors. Do they? The fact that CEOs who are appointed *before* the appointment of their compensation committee chairs are paid more, on average, than CEOs who are appointed *after* suggests that they do (Main et al., 1995). Examining the composition of boards of directors more carefully, we see that, in general, directors may be informed, but they are not independent.

Three factors compromise directors' independence from their CEOs. The first is gratitude. The board member's job is prestigious, lucrative, and undemanding. Directors of the 200 largest American corporations receive on average $179,000 for 20 days of work per year (Schellhardt, 1999; Jaffe, 2003). They may also be given life and medical insurance, retirement benefits, and the use of company property such as automobiles and vacation homes (Main et al., 1995). In addition, there is the considerable "social capital" directors acquire in the form of connections with influential people. Thus getting an appointment to a board is like getting a large gift. This is problematic, for it is natural for gift-recipients to feel grateful to gift-givers. The larger the gift is, the more grateful, and more inclined to "return the favor," the gift-recipient will be. Since CEOs have a great deal of influence over who gets appointed to the board, the directors will feel grateful to him. To represent properly shareholders' interests, then, they will have to fight against this feeling (Crystal, 1991; Nichols & Subramanian, 2001). There is reason

to believe they have not been successful. Recent research shows a positive correlation between director and CEO pay (Boyd, 1994).[4]

Self-interest is the second factor compromising the independence of directors in
pay negotiations with CEOs. To determine how much to pay their CEO, the board
will usually find out how much CEOs of comparable firms are being paid (Porac
et al., 1999). The more those CEOs make, the more the board will pay their CEO
(O'Reilly et al., 1988; Ezzamel & Watson, 1998). The problem is that many boards
have members who are CEOs of comparable firms (Kesner, 1988; O'Reilly et al.,
1988; Main et al., 1995). This is good from the point of view of having knowl-
edgeable directors. But CEO-directors have a self-interested reason to increase the
pay of the CEO with whom they are negotiating. Suppose CEO A sits on CEO B's
board, and A and B run comparable firms. The more pay A agrees to give to B, the
more pay A himself will later receive. For, when it is time to determine A's pay
package, B's pay package will be used as one of the reference points.

The third factor is not a reason directors have to favor CEOs; it is the absence of a
reason directors should have to favor shareholders. Since they are paying with their
own money, shareholders have a powerful incentive not to overpay the CEO. The
more they pay the CEO, the less they have for themselves. Directors, by contrast, are
not paying with their own money. Although they are often given shares in the company as compensation, directors are rarely required to buy them (Hambrick &
Jackson, 2000; Daily & Dalton, 2003). So their incentive not to overpay the CEO is
less powerful. It might be wondered whether shareholders can make it more powerful by threatening to recall overly generous directors. They cannot. Shareholders in
most firms lack this power. In fact, not only will directors have nothing to fear if they
do overpay the CEO, they will have something to fear if they *do not*. Shareholders
cannot recall generous directors, but CEOs can use their power to force them out.

To sum up, according to the agreement view, a wage of $8 million per year is
just if and only if it results from an arm's-length negotiation between an informed
CEO and an informed group of owners. We argued that these negotiations are
not, in general, conducted at arm's-length. It follows that $8 million per year is not
a just (average) wage. Because the independence condition is violated in a way that
favors the CEO, we can be confident that the just average wage on this view is less
than $8 million per year. Speculation about how much less, however, would be
premature. A different view of justice in wages may be correct, and it may justify
the current level of CEO pay. The next section will examine the desert view.

---

[4] This contradicts the intuitively plausible view that, since most directors are rich already, the money
they get paid for being a director will not influence them.

The Desert View

A familiar complaint about CEO pay is that it has increased in years when firms have performed badly. This complaint is grounded in the desert view of justice in wages. It assumes that a CEO should get the wages he deserves, that the wages a CEO deserves is determined by his contribution to the firm, and that the proper measure of contribution is firm performance. If the firm performs worse in year two than in year one, the argument goes, the CEO deserves to make less, and therefore should make less, in year two than in year one. The agreement and utility views of justice in wages cannot account, except indirectly, for this intuition.[5]

Determining how much pay CEOs deserve involves us in two difficulties. The first is identifying the standard(s) for deservingness. One cannot be deserving for no reason at all; desert requires a basis (Feinberg, 1970; Feldman, 1995). As noted above economic contribution is often taken to be the basis of desert of wages (Feinberg, 1973; Miller, 1989, 1999). But others have been offered as well, including (1) the physical effort exerted by the worker (Sadurski, 1985), (2) the amount of ability, skill, or training his job requires (Nagel, 1979), (3) its difficulty, stress, dangerousness, or unpleasantness (Feinberg, 1970; Sher, 1987), and (4) its degree of responsibility or importance (Soltan, 1987). Desert may be determined by one or several of these factors. The second problem is connected to the first. Once we identify the base(s) for desert of wages, then we must find a way of matching desert levels to pay levels. Suppose contribution is the basis of desert, and suppose, as a direct result of key decisions by the CEO, the firm's profits increase 20% in a year. We might think that the CEO's desert-level increases by 20%, and therefore that he deserves a 20% raise. But what should his initial salary have been? Without a way of matching desert levels to pay levels, we cannot answer this question. However, from the point of view of desert, the absolute amount of the CEO's pay raise matters as much as its percentage increases.[6]

---

[5] Most researchers believe CEO pay is not, in fact, tied closely to performance. See, for example, Baker et al. (1988), Jensen and Murphy (1990), and Kerr and Bettis (1987). For opposing views, see Hall and Liebman (1998) and Haubrich (1994).

[6] Some theorists ignore this. Murphy's (1986) argument that CEOs are not overpaid relies largely on studies that show a positive correlation between CEO pay and firm performance over time: "for every 10% rise in a company's stock price over [a] ten-year sample, the top executive's salary and bonus rose an average of 1.1%" (1986: 127). This is at most half of what needs to be proven. We must consider not just the percentage increase in CEO pay but its absolute amount.

In this chapter, both of these problems are avoided. The first questions our ability to identify the base(s) of desert. In response, I will assume, as most parties to the debate about CEO pay do, that the basis for desert of pay is contribution. Indeed, of all the desert-bases mentioned above, this is the one most likely to justify the current level of CEO pay. The second questions our ability to identify what it is exactly that people deserve. In response, I will not argue that CEOs deserve to make less than $8 million per year *absolutely*. Instead, I will argue that that they deserve to make less than $8 million per year *given that* their employees make on average $27,000 per year. CEOs are not 301 times as deserving as their employees.

Under the assumption that contribution is the sole desert-base for pay, the CEO deserves to be paid 301 times what the average worker is paid if and only if his contribution is 301 times as valuable as the worker's. For every $1 in revenue the worker generates, the CEO must generate $301. If the worker generates $100,000 in a year, the CEO must generate $30.1 million. Does this happen?

Some will deny that this question can be answered. They will say that employees are not Robinson Crusoes, each at work on their own self-contained projects. Instead, many people work together on the same complex projects. As a result, it is difficult or impossible to tell where one person's contribution ends and another's begins (Goodin, 1985; Anderson, 1999; Scheffler, 2000).

This is not, of course, an objection that will be advanced by those who appeal to the desert view to justify the current level of CEO pay. They need a way to measure accurately contribution. If the stronger form of this objection is true, however, and we cannot tell how much each employee contributes to the firm, then we cannot tell how much each deserves to be paid. So this conclusion is not unwelcome from the point of view of this chapter, but it is weak. A thoroughgoing skepticism about the accuracy of contribution measurements yields the conclusion that we *cannot tell* whether CEOs deserve to make 301 times as much as their employees, not that they *do not* deserve to make this much. As far as this view is concerned, CEOs may deserve to make *more* than 301 times as much as their employees do.

This kind of skepticism about the accuracy of contribution measurements is, I believe, unwarranted. Although it may be impossible to determine exactly how much each employee contributes to the firm, rough estimates are possible. The popular view, of course, is that CEOs matter enormously to their firms. The CEOs of successful corporations are glorified in news stories and biographies. Witness, for example, the flurry of books written by and about Jack Welch, the former chief executive of General Electric. If we accept this view, we will conclude that CEOs' contributions are at least 301 times as valuable as their employees'.

But we should not. To be sure, some scholars endorse the popular view (Weiner & Mahoney, 1981; Smith et al., 1984; Kotter, 1988; Shamir et al., 1993). But an increasing number reject it (Lieberson & O'Connor, 1972; Pfeffer & Salancik, 1978; Hannan & Freeman, 1989; Carroll & Hannan, 2000).[7] Summarizing the current state of the debate, Khurana says the "overall evidence" points to "at best a contingent and relatively minor cause-and-effect relationship between CEOs and firm performance . . ." (2002: 23). He explains: "a variety of internal and external constraints inhibit CEOs' abilities to affect firm perform-ance . . . [including] internal politics, previous investments in fixed assets and par-ticular markets, organizational norms, and external forces such as competitive pressures and barriers to exit and entry" (2002: 22). It cannot be denied that CEOs' decisions at times make a difference to firm performance. These leaders may deserve bonuses for strategic thinking. But, if Khurana is right, cases such as these are exceptions to the rule. Factors outside of the CEO's control normally "contribute" more to the firm's success than the CEO does.

Some will reject the research on which this result is founded. Others will point out that it is compatible with the claim that CEOs contribute 301 times as much to their firms as their employees. These claims are not irrational. No theorist is willing to say exactly how much, compared to the average employee, the average CEO contributes. But they are unreasonable. There is mounting evidence that CEOs are not as important as they were once thought to be, and that average employees are far from useless. We have ample evidence for a negative conclusion; the claim that CEOs deserve to be paid 301 times as much as their employees is *unjustified*. But I think the evidence licenses a tentative positive conclusion as well; CEOs are *less* than 301 times as deserving as their employees, and so deserve *less* than 301 times as much pay. The desert view clearly does not support, and probably condemns, the current level of CEO pay.

The Utility View

Having considered the agreement and desert views of justice in wages, let us now turn to the utility view. To recall, this view says that a just wage for a CEO is one

---

[7] Even those who think leadership matters acknowledge its limited significance. Thomas says that "leader differences do account for performance variables within firms to a substantial degree, [but] . . . these impacts are generally insufficient to outweigh the inbuilt differences among firms that largely account for performance variation among firms" (1988: 399).

that maximizes firm wealth by attracting, retaining, and motivating a talented leader. This is perhaps the most important of the three views of justice in wages. Boards of directors frequently appeal to utility-based arguments to defend the pay packages they give to their CEOs (Zajac & Westphal, 1995; Wade et al., 1997). I will argue that these defenses fail. I begin by discussing pay as a tool of attraction and retention. I then consider its role in motivation.

Attraction and Retention

Several of the desert-bases discussed above might be cited as reasons an employer has to pay more to fill a certain job. The most important of these are effort, skill, and difficulty (including stress, dangerousness, and unpleasantness).[8] Since, other things being equal, an employee will choose an easier job over a harder job, employers will have to make other things unequal, by offering higher wages for the harder job. Similarly, employers will offer higher wages for jobs that require rare and valuable skills or long periods of training, and for jobs that are comparatively difficult.[9]

The CEO's job has some of these characteristics. It does not require much physical effort, but it requires skill and training, and it is difficult and stressful. According to one study (Kudo et al., 1988), CEOs work on average 13 h per day. The question, of course, is not *if* the CEO's job has these characteristics, but *to what degree* it has them. Is the CEO's job *so* difficult and stressful, and does it require *so* much skill and training, that offering $8 million per year is necessary to get talented people to become CEOs? Those convinced by my argument that CEOs do not deserve to be paid 301 times what their employees are paid may think not. But notice we are now asking a different question: not what people deserve for performing the CEO's job, but what would make them willing to perform it.

The answer, however, is similar. There is no evidence that offering $8 million per year is necessary to get talented people to become CEOs (Milkovich & Rabin,

---

[8] I do not include on this list degree of responsibility. While some people may not want to hold jobs in which they could have a significant impact on people's lives, I suspect there are equally many, if not more, who do. I also do not include contribution. Instead I understand "skill" expansively to include all of the talents and traits taken by firms to be positively correlated with contribution.

[9] Nichols and Subramanian (2001) suggest that high CEO pay is justified, in part, because CEOs' jobs are risky. When the company performs poorly, CEOs are more likely than average workers to be fired. But this ignores the fact that CEOs have less to fear from job loss than average workers. CEOs are wealthy, whereas most employees cannot afford to be out of work for long.

1991). Indeed, we have reason to believe that much less will do. Consider the jobs of university presidents and US military generals. They are no less difficult, and require no less skill and training, than the jobs of CEOs. But the wages offered to presidents and generals are many times lower than the wages offered to CEOs. The median compensation of presidents of private research universities is $385,000 (Basinger, 2003); US military generals earn $143,000 per year (Bureau of Labor Statistics, 2004). Despite this, there is no shortage of talented university presidents and military generals. The fact that people can be attracted to difficult, specialized, and high-skill managerial jobs that pay "only" several hundred thousand dollars per year suggests that talented people will still want to become CEOs even if they are paid less than $8 million per year.

Three objections might be advanced against this conclusion. It might be admitted that the CEO's job is about as difficult, and requires about as much skill and training, as the university president's job or the military general's job. But, it might be said, the CEO's job is in one important way more unpleasant than these jobs. Military generals get, in addition to a paycheck, the satisfaction of knowing that they are protecting their country. University presidents get, in addition to a paycheck, the satisfaction of knowing that they are helping to increase human understanding. There is no comparable benefit, according to this objection, for CEOs.

I suspect that many CEOs find their jobs immensely intrinsically rewarding, and would find this suggestion mildly insulting. But let us grant, for the sake of argument, that CEOs' jobs are less intrinsically rewarding than university presidents' and military generals' jobs. Are they *that* much less rewarding – as many as 21 times so? For the objection to succeed, they would have to be. But it is implausible to suppose that they are. While the extra unpleasantness of the CEO's job may make it necessary to offer more than $385,000 per year to attract talented candidates, it is hardly plausible to suppose that it makes it necessary to offer $8 million.

The second objection grants that talented people would still be attracted to the CEO's job even if they were offered less than $8 million per year. But, it says, when this much pay is offered, truly exceptional people become interested. Analogously, the people who are now university presidents are talented, but truly exceptional people would become university presidents if they were offered, instead of several hundred thousand dollars per year, several million dollars per year.

Pay does matter to people when they are choosing a profession (Freeman, 1971; Bok, 1993). So it is reasonable to assume that the people who become CEOs because corporations offer $8 million per year are, on average, more talented than the people who would become CEOs if corporations offered $1 million per year. But there are two reasons to think that they are not *that much* more talented, and so not worth the extra pay. First, the spectrum of managerial talent is only so wide. And $1 million per year is more than enough to attract a talented person to a difficult and important managerial job, as is demonstrated by the high talent level found among military generals and university presidents. Thus, the $8 million-per-year CEO simply *cannot be* that much more talented than the $1 million-per-year CEO. Second, as we said above, firms' performances do not usually depend heavily on the contributions of their CEOs. So it is unlikely that the modest difference in talent between the $8-million-per-year-CEO and the $1-million-per-year-CEO will translate into a $7 million difference in firm performance. In support of this, note that while American CEOs significantly outearn Japanese and British CEOs, American firms do not generally outperform Japanese and British firms (Abowd & Kaplan, 1999).

It might be said – as a third objection – that I am missing the point. The fact is that the going rate *now* for CEOs is $8 million per year. In this market, it is necessary for any one firm to offer $8 million per year to get a talented person to become its CEO (Ezzamel & Watson, 1998). This argument defies free market economic sense. It says, in effect, that the market cannot correct itself. This is pessimistic.

Our discussion has focused on attraction; we have said nothing about retention. Could it be the case that, while $8 million per year is not necessary to *attract* talented people to the CEO's job, it is necessary to *retain* them in the face of competing offers? The answer is no. In the first place, it is unlikely that there will be many competing offers. According to a study by Challenger, Gray and Christmas, Inc., of the 67 CEO departures in December 2003, in only one case was "position elsewhere" given as the reason for the departure. If CEOs were paid less, this number might increase. But even if it did, firms should not be alarmed. The difficulty of retention is a function of the difficulty of attraction. If it is not difficult to get a qualified person to take the CEO's job in the first place, it will not be difficult – or, more to the point, necessary – to retain him in the face of competing offers. The company can simply hire a new one.[10]

---

[10] This is not to suggest that companies should make *no* effort to keep their CEOs. There is debate about whether CEO succession events disrupt firm performance, but most writers agree that they tend to lower the price of the firm's stock (Beatty & Zajac, 1987).

Motivation

Attraction and retention are not the only utility-based reasons for paying employees certain wages. There is also motivation. Employees who are talented *and* motivated create more wealth for their firms than employees who are only talented. There are three ways in which paying CEOs $8 million per year might be thought – mistakenly, I will argue – to maximize firm wealth through motivation.

First, it might motivate the CEO himself. The CEO knows that, if he does not do an excellent job, he will be fired. Since he wants to keep making $8 million per year, he will work as hard as he can. If CEOs were paid less money, they would work less hard, and firms would be worse off.

In this respect also, pay matters; it motivates people to work hard (Abowd, 1990; Leonard, 1990; Lawler, 1991). It is thus arguable that the CEO who is paid $8 million per year will work harder than the CEO who is paid $1 million per year. But this, as we know by now, is not what needs to be shown. What needs to be shown is that the extra amount of hard work put in by the $8 million-per-year CEO is worth an extra $7 million. It is unlikely that it is. There is no guarantee that extra hard work will translate into extra revenue, and there is only so hard an executive can work. One might think that an extra $7 million per year would be worth it if one thought that CEOs would put in very little effort if they were paid only $1 million per year. But this takes a pessimistic view of CEOs' characters, as if only money – and only a lot of it – could get them to do anything. There is no empirical evidence to support this view (Bok, 1993). To the contrary, studies show that money is not the only, or even the primary, reason people work hard (Freeman, 1971; Annis & Annis, 1986). Instead of trying to further motivate their CEOs with more money, then, firms would do better to use the extra money to increase revenue in other ways, such as advertising more.

The second motivation-based reason for paying CEOs $8 million per year is, in effect, a slightly different version of the first. It has been said that CEOs' compensation packages should be structured so that CEOs' and owners' interests are *aligned* (Jensen & Murphy, 1990; Walters et al., 1995; Nichols & Subramanian, 2001). Owners want the stock price to go up. So CEOs should be paid in a way that makes them want the stock price to go up. This is typically achieved by paying CEOs mostly in restricted stock and stock options. Since, it is assumed, the CEO wants to make more money rather than less, this will give him an incentive to try to make the company's stock price go up. The idea is not just to make sure that CEOs do what investors want, but to make sure that they do *only* what investors want. If the CEO is paid mostly in stock, he has little to gain from pursuing alternative courses of action.

Let us grant, for the sake of argument, that CEOs' interests should be aligned exclusively with investors' interests. Let us also grant that offering CEOs $5 million per year in restricted stock and stock options accomplishes this (Khurana, 2002). Does this prove that CEOs should be paid $5 million in stock? It does only if there is no cheaper way of achieving this goal. But there is: monitoring and dismissal. The interests of most employees are aligned with investors' interests this way. Employees are monitored. If they promote interests other than those (ultimately) of the investors, they are dismissed. Would anyone seriously propose, as an alternative to this practice, giving each employee several million dollars in stock options? To be sure, doing so would align their interests with investors' interests. But it is expensive and unnecessary. The same is true of paying CEOs $5 million in stock. There is no reason to give away so much of the firm's wealth when the CEO can simply be fired for poor performance. Owners could secure the same level of loyalty at a fraction of the price.

We have examined two ways that paying CEOs $8 million per year might maximize firm wealth through motivation. Both focus on the effects of high pay on the CEO. The third focuses on the effects of high pay on other employees. According to some (Lazear & Rosen, 1981; Rosen, 1986; Eriksson, 1999; Bognanno, 2001), a firm's job hierarchy can be seen as a tournament, with the CEO's job as top prize. Many of the firm's employees, they say, want this prize and will work hard to get it. The better the prize is, the harder they will work. If the CEO is paid $8 million per year, the rest of the employees will work very hard indeed. The consequent increase in productivity will be good for the firm as a whole. Ehrenberg and Bognanno (1990) find evidence for this hypothesis in the field of professional golf. They observe that golfers' scores are negatively correlated with potential earnings. The larger the tournament's purse is, and hence the more money the golfers could win, the better they play.

This is the most sophisticated of the utility-based attempts to justify the current level of CEO pay. Still, the argument in its present form has several problems. In the first place, not every employee wants to be CEO, no matter how much the job pays. So paying the CEO $8 million per year provides an incentive to work hard to only some of the firm's employees. Second, there is evidence that this practice will have unintended negative effects. Since there is only one CEO's job, employees must compete with each other to get it.[11] The more the job pays,

---

[11] CEOs are increasingly hired from outside the firm. Keiser estimates that, in the years 1960–1964, 3.3% of CEOs "joined their organizations within 2 years of becoming CEO" (2004: 63). In 1985–1989, the number was 28%. This complicates, but does not undermine, my argument. New CEOs have to come from *somewhere*. If a lower-level manager does not become the CEO at his present firm, he has an opportunity to become the CEO elsewhere.

the more intense the competition will be. This is problematic, for competition fosters jealousy and hostility, which can hinder communication and cooperation (Meyer, 1975; Lawler, 1981; Annis & Annis, 1986). This will not matter to golfers; they play alone. But employees often work together; a decline in communication and cooperation may lead to a decline in productivity. In support of this, Cowherd and Levine (1992) find that pay inequality between workers and managers is negatively correlated with product quality. Thus, while paying CEOs $8 million per year may increase hard work, it may also increase competition. The benefit of the former may be outweighed by the cost of the latter.

Even if it is not, this does not suffice to prove that CEOs should be paid $8 million per year. My objection is familiar. That is, while paying CEOs $8 million per year might be an effective motivational tool, it is likely not a *cost-effective* one. Above, we said that the $8-million-per-year CEO is likely to be only slightly more productive than the $1-million-per-year CEO. Similar reasoning suggests that $8-million-per-year CEO hopefuls are likely to be only slightly more productive than $1-million-per-year CEO hopefuls. From the point of view of utility, then, firms would do better to use the extra $7 million to increase revenue in other ways.

Conclusion

To structure the debate about executive compensation, I distinguished three views of justice in wages: the agreement view, the desert view, and the utility view. No matter which one is right, I argued, CEO pay is too high. Owners may "agree" to pay CEOs $8 million per year, but the negotiations are not conducted at arm's-length. If they were, CEOs would be paid less. The evidence also suggests that CEOs do not deserve to make 301 times what workers make, and that paying CEOs $8 million per year does not maximize firm wealth. New evidence may emerge that challenges these conclusions. Alternatively, new theories of justice in wages may be developed. Until then, it is reasonable to believe that CEO pay is too high.

This result is important. It supports the popular suspicion that CEOs are overpaid. But our inquiry leaves an important question unanswered, namely, exactly how much should CEOs be paid? Answering this question will truly be an interdisciplinary effort. First, we must determine what the correct view of justice in wages is. That is, we must determine which of the values, in this context, is most important. Here the writings of moral and political philosophers will be relevant. Second, we must apply the correct theory of justice in wages to the problem of CEO pay. That is, we must identify the wage that maximizes firm wealth, gives the CEO what he deserves, or would be the result of an arm's-length negotiation between the CEO and the owners. Here the writings of economists and organizational theorists will be relevant. Each of these tasks will be difficult and will require a full discussion of its own. In the meantime, what should be done? CEO pay should be kept from increasing; ideally, it should decrease. Space considerations prevent a detailed discussion of how this can be accomplished. I conclude, however, with two preliminary suggestions.

First, CEOs should be removed from the director election process. Directors feel obligated to those who put them on the board. If this is the CEO, they will feel obligated to him, and be more inclined to overpay him. Directors should feel obligated to the people they are actually representing: the shareholders. Letting shareholders elect them will help to create this feeling. It is possible that it will also make being a director a more demanding job. It may end the era in which an individual can serve on several corporate boards and still hold a full time job. This would be a good thing. Being a director is an important job: directors oversee entities whose actions can impact the welfare of thousands of people. It should feel like one.

Second, directors should be required to make meaningful investments in the firms that they direct. They need not all own a certain percentage of the firm's total stock. What matters is that they own an amount that is meaningful for them (Hambrick & Jackson, 2000). This promotes the first objective: directors will feel more obligated to shareholders if they are themselves shareholders. It is useful for another reason as well. We said earlier that a problem with the pay negotiations between directors and CEOs is that directors feel as if they are not paying with their own money. Making them buy stock would help to ameliorate this problem (Boyd, 1994). An implication of this view is that other kinds of compensation that seem "free" to directors should be eliminated. This includes stock options insofar as they are not counted against firm earnings. If options are given as compensation, they should be expensed.

ACKNOWLEDGMENTS

A draft of this chapter was presented as a paper at Georgetown University. I wish to thank members of that audience, and also George Brenkert, Edwin Hartman, Kelly Moriarty, Jeffrey Wilder, and two anonymous *Business Ethics Quarterly* referees for helpful comments and discussion.

REFERENCES

Abowd, J. M. 1990. Does performance-based compensation affect corporate performance? *Industrial and Labor Relations Review*, **43**: 52S–73S.

Abowd, J. M. and Kaplan, D. S. 1999. Executive compensation: six questions that need answering. *Journal of Economic Perspectives*, **13**: 145–168.

Anderson, E. 1999. What is the point of equality? *Ethics*, **109**: 287–337.

Annis, D. B. and Annis, L. F. 1986. Merit pay, utilitarianism, and desert. *Journal of Applied Philosophy*, **3**: 33–41.

Baker, G. P., Jensen, M. C., and Murphy, K. L. 1988. Compensation and incentives: practice vs. theory. *Journal of Finance*, **43**: 593–616.

Basinger, J. 2003. Soaring pay, big questions. *Chronicle of Higher Education*, **50** (12): S9–S11.

Beatty, R. P. and Zajac, E. J. 1987. CEO change and firm performance in large corporations: succession effects and manager effects. *Strategic Management Journal*, **8**: 305–317.

Bognanno, M. L. 2001. Corporate tournaments. *Journal of Labor Economics*, **19**: 290–315.

Bok, D. C. 1993. *The Cost of Talent*. New York: Free Press.

Boyd, B. K. 1994. Board control and CEO compensation. *Strategic Management Journal*, **15**: 335–344.

Bureau of Labor Statistics. 2004. *Occupational Outlook Handbook, 2004–05 Edition*. Washington, DC: US Department of Labor.

Byrne, J. A. 2002. How to fix corporate governance. *Business Week*, May 6: 68–75.

Carroll, G. and Hannan, M. T. 2000. *The Demography of Corporations and Industries*. Princeton, NJ: Princeton University Press.

Cowherd, D. M. and Levine, D. I. 1992. Product quality and pay equity between lower-level employees and top management: an investigation of distributive justice theory. *Administrative Science Quarterly*, **37**: 302–320.

Crystal, G. S. 1991. *In Search of Excess*. New York: Norton.

Daily, C. M. and Dalton, D. R. 2003. Are director equity policies exclusionary? *Business Ethics Quarterly*, **13**: 415–432.

Ehrenberg, R. and Bognanno, M. L. 1990. Do tournaments have incentive effects? *Journal of Political Economy*, **98**: 1307–1324.

Eriksson, T. 1999. Executive compensation and tournament theory: empirical tests on Danish data. *Journal of Labor Economics*, **17**: 262–280.

Ezzamel, M. and Watson, R. 1998. Market comparison earnings and the bidding-up of executive cash compensation: evidence from the United Kingdom. *Academy of Management Journal*, **41**: 221–231.

Feinberg, J. 1970. *Doing and Deserving*. Princeton, NJ: Princeton University Press.

Feinberg, J. 1973. *Social Philosophy*. Englewood Cliffs, NJ: Prentice-Hall.

Feldman, F. 1995. Desert: reconsideration of some received wisdom. *Mind*, **104**: 63–77.

Freeman, R. 1971. *The Market for College-Trained Manpower*. Cambridge, MA: Harvard University Press.

Goodin, R. 1985. Negating positive desert claims. *Political Theory*, **13**: 575–598.

Hall, B. J. and Liebman, J. B. 1998. Are CEOs really paid like bureaucrats? *Quarterly Journal of Economics*, **111**: 653–691.

Hambrick, D. C. and Jackson, E. M. 2000. Outside directors with a stake: the linchpin in improving governance. *California Management Review*, **42** (4): 108–127.

Hannan, M. T. and Freeman, J. 1989. *Organizational Ecology*. Cambridge, MA: Harvard University Press.

Haubrich, J. G. 1994. Risk aversion, performance pay, and the principal-agent problem. *Journal of Political Economy*, **102**: 258–276.

Jaffe, M. 2003. Average CEO pay at big firms held steady at $11.3 million. *The Mercury News*. December 30. On the internet at: http://www.mercurynews.com/mld/mercurynews/business/7597346.htm.

Jensen, M. C. and Murphy, K. J. 1990. Performance pay and top management incentives. *Journal of Political Economy*, **98**: 225–264.

Keiser, J. D. 2004. Chief executives from 1960–1989: a trend toward professionalization. *Journal of Leadership and Organizational Studies*, **10**: 52–68.

Kerr, J. and Bettis, R. A. 1987. Boards of directors, top management compensation, and shareholder returns. *Academy of Management Journal*, **30**: 645–664.

Kesner, I. F. 1988. Directors' characteristics and committee membership: an investigation of type, occupation, tenure, and gender. *Academy of Management Journal*, **31**: 66–84.

Khurana, R. 2002. *Searching for a Corporate Savior: The Irrational Quest for Charismatic CEOs*. Princeton, NJ: Princeton University Press.

Kotter, J. P. 1988. *The Leadership Factor*. New York: The Free Press.

Kudo, H., Tachikawa, T., and Suzuki, N. 1988. How U.S. and Japanese CEO's spend their time. *Long Range Planning*, **21**: 79–82.

Lawler, E. 1991. The organizational impact of executive compensation. In F. Foulkes, ed., *Executive Compensation*. Boston, MA: Harvard Business School Press, pp. 129–151.

Lawler, E. 1981. *Pay and Organizational Development*. Reading, MA: Addison-Wesley.

Lavelle, L. 2004. Executive pay. *Business Week*, April 19: 106–119.

Lazear, E. and Rosen, S. 1981. Rank order tournaments as optimal labor contracts. *Journal of Political Economy*, **89**: 841–864.

Leonard, J. S. 1990. Executive pay and firm performance. *Industrial and Labor Relations Review*, **43**: 13S–29S.

Lieberson, S. and O'Connor, J. F. 1972. Leadership and organizational performance: a study of large corporations. *American Sociological Review*, **37**: 117–130.

Main, B. G., O'Reilly, C. A., and Wade, J. B. 1995. The CEO, the board of directors and executive compensation: economic and psychological perspectives. *Industrial and Corporate Change*, **4**: 292–332.

Meyer, H. H. 1975. The pay-for-performance dilemma. *Organizational Dynamics*, **3**: 39–50.

Miller, D. 1999. *Principles of Social Justice*. Cambridge, MA: Harvard University Press.

Miller, D. 1989. *Market, State, and Community: Theoretical Foundations of Market Socialism*. Oxford: Clarendon Press.

Milkovich, G. T. and Rabin, B. R. 1991. Executive performance and firm performance: research questions and answers. In F. Foulkes, ed., *Executive Compensation*. Boston, MA: Harvard Business School Press.

Murphy, K. J. 1986. Top executives are worth every nickel they get. *Harvard Business Review*, **64** (2): 125–133.

Nagel, T. 1979. *Mortal Questions*. New York: Cambridge University Press.

Nichols, D. and Subramanian, C. 2001. Executive compensation: excessive or equitable? *Journal of Business Ethics*, **29**: 339–351.

O'Reilly III, C. A., Main, B. G., and Crystal, G. S. 1988. CEO compensation as tournament and social comparison: a tale of two theories. *Administrative Science Quarterly*, **33**: 257–274.

Pfeffer, J. and Salancik, G. R. 1978. *The External Control of Organizations*. New York: Harper & Row.

Porac, J. F., Wade, J. B., and Pollock, T. G. 1999. Industry categories and the politics of the comparable firm in CEO compensation. *Administrative Science Quarterly*, **44**: 112–144.

Rosen, S. 1986. Prizes and incentives in elimination tournaments. *American Economic Review*, **76**: 701–715.

Sadurski, W. 1985. *Giving Desert its Due: Social Justice and Legal Theory*. Dordrecht: D. Reidel.

Scheffler, S. 2000. Justice and desert in liberal theory. *California Law Review*, **88**: 965–990.

Schellhardt, T. D. 1999. More directors are raking in six-figure pay. *Wall Street Journal*, October 29: B1.

Shamir, B., House, R. J., and Arthur, M. B. 1993. The motivational effects of charismatic leadership: a self-concept based study. *Organization Science*, **4**: 577–594.

Sher, G. 1987. *Desert*. Princeton, NJ: Princeton University Press.

Shivdasani, A. and Yermack, D. 1999. CEO involvement in the selection of new board members: an empirical analysis. *Journal of Finance*, **54**: 1829–1853.

Smith, J. E., Carson, K. P., and Alexander, R. A. 1984. Leadership: it can make a difference. *Academy of Management Journal*, **27**: 765–776.

Soltan, K. E. 1987. *The Causal Theory of Justice*. Berkeley, CA: University of California Press.

Thomas, A. B. 1988. Does leadership make a difference? *Administrative Science Quarterly*, **33**: 388–400.

Wade, J. B., Porac, J. F., and Pollock, T. G. 1997. Worth, words, and the justification of executive pay. *Journal of Organizational Behavior*, **18**: 641–664.

Walters, B., Hardin, T., and Schick, J. 1995. Top executive compensation: equity or excess? implications for regaining American competitiveness. *Journal of Business Ethics*, **14**: 227–234.

Weiner, N. and Mahoney, T. A. 1981. A model of corporate performance as a function of environmental, organizational, and leadership influences. *Academy of Management Journal*, **24**: 453–470.

Zajac, E. J. and Westphal, J. D. 1995. Accounting for the explanations of CEO compensation: substance and symbolism. *Administrative Science Quarterly*, **40**: 283–308.

11

Executive Compensation:
Just Procedures and Outcomes

Joe DesJardins
College of St. Benedicts/St. John's University, MN

This chapter is a discussion of Chapters 8–10, which give us much to consider: clear analyses, practical advice and recommendations, original and creative perspectives, and careful argumentation. They all agree that the excessive executive compensation that we have witnessed in recent is ethically problematic if not outright inexcusable. The quality of these chapters puts the commentator in a difficult position. In fact, I do not find much with which to argue in any of these chapters. I have a great deal of sympathy with each of them. But perhaps I can advance the discussion by raising some questions or offering some suggestions.

Alston's "The Ethics of Executive Compensation"

I think Alston has done a fine job of identifying a wide range of the problems with the present practice of allowing boards to set CEO compensation packages. He has done a solid job recommending changes in board structure and function that might address many of these problems. I have only two thoughts to add.

First, I think more should be said about the role that consultants and other third parties play in recruiting top executives and advising boards on appropriate compensation packages. Few boards actually conduct the search or negotiate compensation directly and instead rely on "independent" firms to do this work for them. Like the boards themselves, real questions can be raised about the independence of such third parties. In most cases, the consultants are recommended by the company's management, their firms often have prior business relationships with them, and the possibility of future business will depend on the recommendations of management. This suggests that they are not independent of management's interests and that we should examine their role in the process more carefully. As we have witnessed in the accounting and auditing fields, when consultants' livelihood rests in the hands of management, strong incentives are created to lose one's independence and serve only the interests of management. Also, since consultants' fees can be a function of the salaries their candidates receive, a strong incentive is created to "ratchet-up" salary and benefit expectations. Thus, the agency problem reemerges at this point, as well as at the level of management. Finally, many boards are in the position of simply having to trust the consultant's analysis of the "market" for CEOs, making effective negotiation less likely.

Second, I would recommend that Alston not dismiss government action as a source of external regulation so quickly. It seems to me that several regulatory approaches fall far short of the "strong government regulation" that she thinks to be "highly unlikely." I think of Martin Sabo's "The Income Equity Act," which would eliminate all tax deductions for compensations above 25 times of that received by the lowest paid worker in the corporation, or other similar proposals that would remove tax benefits for stock options or direct stock grants. I think neither of these are quite so unlikely, and I think both would go a long way toward controlling run-away CEO compensation packages.

Taylor's "Executive Pay in Public Academia"

This chapter presents a creative approach to the issue of academic executive compensation. There does seem to be something particularly appalling about such high salaries for academic administrators, perhaps especially at public institutions. I also think that there is some sort of internal contradiction involved. But I am not convinced that Taylor's analysis has it quite right.

The key claim for much of Taylor's analysis is that "enhancing autonomy" is one of, if not THE, primary end of public higher education. As Taylor says (p. 142), "The argument of this paper will thus be unpersuasive to persons who believe that the enhancement of autonomy is not the primary aim of higher education." I think he is correct about this.

First, I think much more needs to be said that enhancing the autonomy of "everyone affiliated" with the university is among the university's primary goals. The argument is much more plausible when extended exclusively to students. I am not at all sure that enhancing the autonomy of faculty, for example, is *or should be* a goal of a university. This strikes me as more than a bit paternalistic, in that it seems to assume that the institution is in a better position than I am to take on such a role. Students, perhaps by definition, stand in need of having their autonomy enhanced; I am not so sure about nonstudent employees.

Second, there is an important ambiguity at several points in Taylor's chapter. Is enhancing autonomy "the" primary aim (singular), or "a" primary aim (plural)? I think the distinction is important because I think the argument can work only if it is the singular version. Taylor seems to agree (p. 144). But, I think the singular version is false. As Taylor acknowledges, this may not be true of private institutions of higher education but I also am unconvinced that it is true of public institutions. It is not that I want to claim that there is an "alternative aim," but that there are multiple aims. I think of large land-grant institutions such as my own home state of Minnesota. For example, The University of Minnesota mission statement identifies three equal goals: Research and Discovery; Teaching and Learning; and Outreach and Public Service. Presumably, enhancing autonomy is an essential part of the "teaching and learning" goal, but I would need to see an argument to show how it is an essential part of the research and discovery and outreach and service goals. For Taylor's argument to work, these would all have to be a version of the enhancing autonomy claim, otherwise the door is open for such additional aims to legitimize disproportionate salaries. If university administrators have other fiduciary duties beyond enhancing autonomy, then they have not necessarily breached their fiduciary duty when they accept exorbitant salaries that do not enhance autonomy.

I also wonder how far the argument should be extended. Consider the argument that in order to enhance autonomy, wages and salaries "should be reallocated to such institutions' lower-paid employees." Might not this argument also apply to the disproportionate salaries of faculty and staff, and of staff to graduate students and student workers? It would seem that the ultimate conclusion of this argument is that all salaries should be equal. If so, then Taylor seems to be committed to the conclusion that there is a direct correlation between income and autonomy. If not, then more needs to be said to explain how unequal incomes can enhance autonomy unequally. Either option has challenges.

First, I am unconvinced that autonomy is the sort of thing that one can measure in the way that it would need to be measured if Professor Taylor's argument is to work. Consider, for example, his claim that the reallocation of salary will enable lower paid employees "to exercise their autonomy to an additional degree that would be greater than any consequent diminution in the ability of the former to exercise theirs" (p. 147). This suggests a sort of utilitarian calculus for autonomy. One ought to distribute income (at least in the zero-sum world of public universities) in whichever way this will result in an optimal enhancement of autonomy. Presumably, if enhancing autonomy is "the" primary aim for universities, similar arguments could be made for any university policy: one ought to do whatever will result in a net increase in the ability to exercise autonomy. But for this to have any practical implications at all, one would need a way to measure and compare the enhancement of autonomy. I simply do not know how this could ever be done.

I also think the connection between income and autonomy needs to be spelled out more fully. Might it be the case, for example, that the autonomy of senior administrators would be enhanced more than the autonomy of lower-paid workers by an equal increase in salary? Taylor assumes without argument that there is a diminishing rate of return on autonomy as income increases. But why cannot the marginal increase in the enhancement of autonomy of senior administrators that would be accomplished by a transfer of wealth from lower-paid workers be greater than the parallel increase accomplished by a transfer from administrators to other workers?

Finally, and connected to this, is the possibility that greater income might actually lead to a diminution of autonomy rather than to an increase. Consider the voluntary simplicity movement and the corresponding critique of consumerism. I am thinking of people such as Juliet Shor who argue that there is good empirical evidence that at least some consumers are caught up in a cycle of work and spend that leads to both an increase in income and a loss of control (and happiness). I do think that the connection between income and autonomy is an empirical relationship and, therefore, we need to know more about the claim that autonomy is enhanced when income in increased.

Moriarty's "How to (Try to) Justify CEO Pay"

I also have a great deal of sympathy with Professor Moriarty's chapter. Allow me to raise two issues that are less criticisms than they are questions for future discussion.

First, as I read this chapter, the counterargument to the "agreement view" is that boards are not in fact independent of the CEOs with whom they enter into agreement. We are told (p. 158) that an agreement is just "if and only if" the agreement "results from an arms-length negotiation between an informed CEO and an informed group of owners." I can accept the initial "if" (the necessary condition) but I am not yet convinced of the "only if" (the sufficient condition). The lack of independence shows an apparent conflict of interest (which itself is an ethical concern), but it need not make the agreement unjust. We may have reason to be skeptical of such agreements, and examine them carefully, but arguments need to be developed to prove that they are necessarily unjust. Much of the discussion surrounding executive compensation shares this assumption but, we need arguments to show that lack of independence necessarily results in an unjust or inefficient agreement.

My second question arose from an example that remained in my mind as I read this chapter. In trying to distinguish the three views, I think about contingency fees that many lawyers charge their clients. These sometimes result in seemingly outrageous payments to lawyers at the conclusion of a successful lawsuit. (A contingency fee occurs when a client approaches an attorney who agrees to accept a case for a percentage of any settlement, thus the fee is contingent upon winning the case.) This seems to have elements of all three: there was an agreement, the potential payment offers great incentives for future work, and, given victory, the fee would be deserved for successful work. I wonder if this model, which combines Moriarty's three types, might provide us with the strongest rationale for executive compensation.

In considering this example, I also was reminded of a claim once made by Al "Chainsaw" Dunlap. Dunlap was unapologetic about the multimillion dollar salary he had just received from Scott Paper. The salary represented a very small percentage of the increase in stockholder wealth that had been created by his policies and decisions. That wealth would not have existed had it not been for his leadership. It was also the agreement that he made going into a situation in which he was asked to turnaround Scott Paper's prospects. Because this was the agreement going in, and since both sides were aware of the risks but were willing to accept them as an incentive, the outcome was deserved. Being paid a small percentage of the marginal increase was, according to Dunlap, fair all around.

I am not sure what to say about contingency fees for attorneys. My intuition is that they are fair and just. Individual clients entering into such agreements may be under stress and may prefer not to accept paying such high fees, but I do not think the agreement is coerced. I believe it meets the standard of informed consent. I also think that, to a large extend, the attorney's work is a *sine qua non*, for the settlement, and therefore is deserved. I also think that they do provide great motivation, although admittedly, equal motivation might be provided by alternative arrangements.

My question, therefore, concerns a parallel case with CEO pay. If, in fact, shareholder wealth is increased significantly, and if this was the prior agreement, and if the CEO's work was an essential element in this increase, why should we not allow the possibility that some CEO salaries are justified by the agreement made with the firm? I think some boards may well view the compensation package as the type of wager that a client makes with an attorney who takes on her case.

Surely there are some dissimilarities. We have seen solid empirical evidence that suggests CEOs are not the *sin qua non* for corporate success in the way that a good attorney might be for legal victory. Repricing stock options and renegotiating executive compensations may also make CEO pay less risky than attorney's fees. Attorneys are less able to manipulate the legal outcome than CEOs are able to manipulate earnings. But these strike me more as practical problems and challenges in insuring that the model is appropriately enforced, than in-principle objections to the ethics of the model.

INDEX

Page numbers in *italics* refer to illustrations

Printed and bound by CPI Group (UK) Ltd, Croydon, CR0 4YY

16/04/2025

14658821-0004